SEMINAR STUDIES IN HISTORY

Gladstone, Disraeli
and Later
Victorian Politics
Second Edition

SEMINAR STUDIES IN HISTORY

A full list of titles in the series
will be found on the back cover
of this book.

SEMINAR STUDIES IN HISTORY
General Editor: Roger Lockyer

Gladstone, Disraeli and Later Victorian Politics

Second Edition

Paul Adelman

Reader in History,
Kingston Polytechnic, Surrey

LONGMAN

LONGMAN GROUP UK LIMITED
*Longman House, Burnt Mill, Harlow, Essex CM20 2JE, England
and Associated Companies throughout the World.*

© Longman Group Limited 1970, 1983

First published 1970
Ninth impression 1991

ISBN 0 582 35332 7

Set in 10/11pt. Baskerville, Linotron 202

Printed in Malaysia
by Vinlin Press Sdn. Bhd.,
Sri Petaling, Kuala Lumpur

Cover: Mansell Collection

For David

Contents

Seminar Studies in History
Founding Editor: Patrick Richardson

Introduction

The Seminar Studies series was conceived by Patrick Richardson, whose experience of teaching history persuaded him of the need for something more substantial than a textbook chapter but less formidable than the specialised full-length academic work. He was also convinced that such studies, although limited in length, should provide an up-to-date and authoritative introduction to the topic under discussion as well as a selection of relevant documents and a comprehensive bibliography.

Patrick Richardson died in 1979, but by that time the Seminar Studies series was firmly established, and it continues to fulfil the role he intended for it. This book, like others in the series, is therefore a living tribute to a gifted and original teacher.

Note on the System of References:
A bold number in round brackets (**5**) in the text refers the reader to the corresponding entry in the Bibliography section at the end of the book. A bold number in square brackets, preceded by 'doc' [**docs 6, 8**] refers the reader to the corresponding items in the section of Documents, which follows the main text.

ROGER LOCKYER
General Editor

Foreword

The period between 1867 and the death of Queen Victoria in 1901 saw the development of the major features of the modern British political system, features which, in their essentials, still govern our political life today. It was during this period that the Second and Third Reform Acts of 1867 and 1884 established the principle of 'one man, one vote' and thus inaugurated the era of democratic politics; while the Redistribution Act of 1885, by dividing up the country into one-member constituencies roughly equal in population, destroyed the old parliamentary map of Britain, and laid down the main outlines of the present constituency system. These changes in the electoral system at the centre were underpinned by the 'democratisation' of local government by the great acts of 1888 and 1894. Nor was electoral procedure left untouched. Corruption, bribery and influence had long disgraced the electoral scene even after the passing of the Second Reform Act, and despite the introduction of the secret ballot in 1872. But the passing of a rigorous Corrupt Practices Act in 1883 did much to destroy the evils of the old order, and helped to produce an electoral system that, within a generation, was reasonably fair and honest.

Above all, however, the period between 1867 and 1901 saw the development of the two-party system, associated with the 'swing of the pendulum' between the Liberal and Conservative (and later the Labour and Conservative) parties, that many people came to see as the essential and characteristic feature of modern British politics. It was this system too that produced and nourished the political giants of the age – Gladstone, Disraeli, Chamberlain, Salisbury – and helped to establish their hold over the political imagination of the British people, both then and since. But the Liberal and Conservative Parties in the later Victorian period were not just parliamentary organisations. Faced, after 1867, with the problem of winning working-class votes, both parties developed central organisations whose tasks – raising money, encouraging voluntary workers, finding suitable parliamentary candidates – were basically what they are today; while at the same time local constituency associations were developed which still remain important centres of local political life. Moreover, the federation of these local associations into great national organisations – the Conservative National Union of 1867, and the National Liberal Federation of 1877 – raised in an acute form the problem of the relationship between the parliamentary parties and extra-parliamentary opinion; a problem which, though scotched by the party leaders in the later nineteenth century, has recently emerged in a more virulent form to tax their successors.

This book is an attempt to describe the development of that later Victorian political system. It is concerned primarily with the two great parties, Liberal and Conservative, considered mainly as political organisations – vote-winning agencies – rather than as repositories of political ideas or vehicles of legislative change. It discusses, therefore, such problems as: how were the parties organised, who supported them and why, what factors divided and united them, what was the influence of leadership and policy upon their development, how successful or unsuccessful were they at general elections and why? This is not to deny the role of ideas in history or to insist that politics is just organisation; but it is an attempt to provide a guiding thread through a mass of historical detail, and to draw attention to aspects of nineteenth-century history which have received scant attention in the textbooks. For indeed it is in the field of party history in the later nineteenth century that some of the most interesting and fruitful work has been done by British and American historians in the last twenty years. Unfortunately, though, no general survey of the years 1867 to 1901 has been produced by a professional historian since R. C. K. Ensor published his *England 1870–1914* in 1936. This makes the study of the period challenging, but also, I believe, particularly rewarding for students, and especially well adapted to the seminar method of study.

Many of the topics dealt with in this book are the concern of social scientists as well as historians. But this is intended to be an historical study. Though I have not, I hope, neglected the work of sociologists and political scientists, I have made no attempt to apply sociological 'theories' to the political world of the late Victorians. I have allowed the Victorians – the great and the insignificant – to speak for themselves; the student must draw his own conclusions.

Paul Adelman, 1970

Note on the Second Edition

I have taken the opportunity of a second edition to correct misprints and inaccuracies in the original text, and to expand on some points where brevity displaced understanding. My main purpose, however, has been to update the book in terms of the scholarship of the past decade, years which have seen the continuing publication of important works on later Victorian politics. The decade has on the whole been one of consolidation rather than of pioneering in historical writing. This is recognised by the recent publication of two new general surveys of the period by Professors Shannon and Read to complement Ensor's classic textbook which (as my original Foreword records) for so long held the field.

Paul Adelman, 1982

Acknowledgements

We are grateful to the following for permission to reproduce copyright material:
George Allen and Unwin Limited for an extract from *English Radicalism 1886–1914* by Simon Maccoby; American Historical Association for an extract from 'The Introduction of Industrialists into the British Peerage' by Ralph E. Pumphrey from *American Historical Review*, Vol. 32, 1959–60; G. Bell and Sons Limited for an extract from 'The Parliamentary Foundations of the Hotel Cecil' by J. P. Cornford from *Ideas and Institutions of Victorian England* edited by Robert Robson; Ernest Benn Limited for an extract from *Imperialism and the Rise of Labour 1895–1905* by Elie Halevy; The Trustees of the British Museum for an extract from Dilke Papers, British Museum ADD Ms, 43898; Cambridge University Press for extracts from *1867 Disraeli, Gladstone and Revolution* by Maurice Cowling, *The Nineteenth Century Constitution* by H. J. Hanham, 'The Politics of the Establishment of County Councils' by J. P. D. Dunbabin from *The Historical Journal*, Vol. 6, 1963 and 'Joseph Chamberlain, the Conservatives and the Succession to John Bright 1886–1889' by M. C. Hurst from *The Historical Journal*, Vol. 7, 1964; the Executors of the Estate of Lady Gwendolen Cecil for extracts from *Life of Robert, Marquis of Salisbury* by Lady Gwendolen Cecil; The Clarendon Press for extracts from *A History of British Trade Unionism Since 1889 Vol. 1, 1889–1910* by Glegg, Fox and Thompson, *England 1870–1914* by Ensor, *Disraeli, Democracy and the Tory Party* by E. J. Feuchtwanger, *The Origins of the Labour Party* by Henry Pelling, *The Political Correspondence of Mr. Gladstone and Lord Glanville 1876–1886* edited by Agatha Ramm and *Ambitions and Strategies* by Peter Stansky; Collins Publishers for an extract from *The Downfall of the Liberal Party* by Trevor Wilson; Columbia University Press for an extract from *The Tariff Reform Movement in Great Britain, 1881–1895* by B. H. Brown; Constable and Company Limited and Charles Scribner's Sons for extracts from *The Formation of the Liberal Party* by John Vincent; Doubleday and Company, Inc for an extract from *Democracy and the Organisation of Political Parties, Vol. 1* by M. Ostrogorski; The Dugdale Society for an extract from *Joseph Chamberlain and West Midland*

Acknowledgements

Politics by M. C. Hurst, Dugdale Society Papers, No. 15; Eyre and Spottiswoode and St. Martin's Press, Inc for extracts from *Disraeli* by Robert Blake; Faber and Faber Limited for an extract from *British Conservatism 1832–1914* by R. B. McDowell; Faber and Faber Limited and Alfred A. Knopf, Inc for extracts from *Modern British Politics* (published in the United States of America as *British Politics in the Collectivist Age*) by Samuel H. Beer; author for an extract from 'English Nonconformists and the Decline of Liberalism' by John F. Glaser from *American Historical Review*, Vol. 36, 1957–8; The Hamlyn Publishing Group Limited for extracts from *Lord Randolph Churchill* by W. S. Churchill and *Joseph Chamberlain, a Political Memoir* edited by C. H. D. Howard; Professor N. G. L. Hammond for extracts from *Gladstone and the Irish Nation* by J. L. Hammond; Heinemann Educational Books Limited and The University of Chicago Press for an extract from *Angels in Marble* by R. McKenzie and A. Silver; the proprietors of *History Today* for an extract from 'Gladstone's Last Cabinet' by the Earl of Rosebery from *History Today*, January 1952; The London School of Economics and Political Science for an extract from *History of Trade Unionism* by Sidney and Beatrice Webb; Macmillan and Company Limited for extracts from *The Government of England* by Lawrence Lowell, *Life of Gladstone* by J. Morley, *The Passing of the Whigs* by Donald Southgate, *Life of Joseph Chamberlain* by J. L. Garvin and Julian Amery, *Social Geography of British Elections 1885–1910* by Henry Pelling, *Popular Politics and Society in Late Victorian Britain* by Henry Pelling and *Labour and Politics 1900–1906* by Frank Bealey and Henry Pelling; John Murray (Publishers) Limited for an extract from *Life of Disraeli* by Buckle and Monypenny; Routledge and Kegan Paul Limited and University of Toronto Press for extracts from *Chief Whip: The Political Life and Times of Aretas Akers-Douglas, First Viscount Chilston* by Viscount Chilston, *Disraelian Conservatism and Social Reform* by Paul Smith, *English Landed Society in the Nineteenth Century* by F. M. L. Thompson and *Socialists, Liberals and Labour: The Struggle for London 1885–1914* by Paul Thompson; the proprietors of *Victorian Studies* for extracts from 'The Transformation of Conservatism in the Late Nineteenth Century' by J. P. Cornford from *Victorian Studies*, VII, 1963–64; Weidenfeld & Nicolson Limited and A. S. Barnes & Company, Inc for an extract from *Lord Randolph Churchill* by R. R. James; Weidenfeld & Nicolson Limited for extracts from *Rosebery* by R. R. James. We have received no objection from Collier-Macmillan International to the use of the extracts from *Rosebery* by R. R. James in the United States of America.

Part One: The Setting

1   Gladstone's Liberal Party

Early development

The origin of the Liberal Party is usually found in the famous meeting held in Willis's rooms on 6 June 1859 when the Whig, Peelite and Radical leaders in Parliament, drawn together by a common sympathy with Italy, agreed to combine together to expel the minority Conservative Government of Derby and Disraeli. As a result a new 'Liberal' ministry was formed under Lord Palmerston which contained for the first time both Mr Gladstone and Lord John Russell. But the government of Lord Palmerston, which lasted for the next six years until his death in October 1865, was still basically only a reconstituted Whig ministry (it contained only one radical) and indeed received the tacit support of the Conservative Party. Two days after Pam's death, however, Disraeli 'foresaw tempestuous times ahead and deep vicissitudes in public life'. Within two years in fact that extension of the suffrage which the old statesman had so long resisted came to pass when, ironically, Disraeli himself introduced the Second Reform Bill in 1867 which eventually granted the vote to the urban working class. At the general election in the following year, the Liberals were swept into power with a majority of more than a hundred, and Gladstone formed his first ministry. The Liberal Party had come of age.

The Parliamentary Liberal Party which thus came into existence in the 1860s, bore all the marks of its origins. It was less a party in the modern sense – organised, disciplined, united around a programme – than a loose alliance of groups of many shades of opinion, reminiscent rather of the parliamentary 'connections' of the age of George III, than of the marshalled party battalions of today. The most famous of these groups, usually regarded as forming the extreme right wing of the party, was the Whigs (**21**). A clique of wealthy aristocratic landowners, easygoing, affable and frank, but suspicious of what they did not understand, the liberalism of the Whig grandees of the period was the product rather of tradition, habit and loyalty than of deeply felt ideas or principles; it is not

I

surprising therefore that it often failed to weather the storms and stresses of an age of rising democracy. Their importance lay not in their numbers, for though they formed a large and important corps in the House of Lords, they numbered hardly more than thirty genuine members in the Lower House in the 1860s; nor in their wealth – which though enormous was hardly tapped at all in the services of the Liberal Party. Their real importance lay in their domination of government – their virtual monopoly of many of the key posts in any Liberal ministry – and the extraordinary esteem of their colleagues and the Parliamentary Party.

At the opposite end of the party's spectrum were the radicals. They too, like the genuine Whigs in the Commons, were a small group – only about fifty members – and probably the most 'crotchety' of all. They contained intellectuals like Henry Fawcett, and John Stuart Mill, who sat briefly for Westminster from 1865 to 1868; but their most important constituent was the great nonconformist manufacturing interest, containing men like Samuel Morley, Titus Salt, William Rathbone and – greatest of all – John Bright, who represented mainly the new industrial constituencies in the North and Midlands. The radical group was the one section of the Liberal Party which was genuinely and passionately committed to challenging the established order in both Church and State; and, in this respect, their greatest obstacle was not so much the glittering but tiny array of Whigs, but the pedestrian mass of moderate Liberals who, neither Whig nor radical, formed the bulk of the membership of the Parliamentary Liberal Party. The moderate Liberals were the ballast which every great parliamentary party must contain. Landowners, lawyers, gentlemen of leisure, army and naval officers, their background and outlook made them distrustful of 'enthusiasm' in either religion or politics, and inclined therefore to be a conservative, but a reasonably openminded, force within the party. On the whole they were content to accept the platitudes of contemporary liberalism and follow the lead of the more distinguished men on the Liberal Front Bench. And indeed this was the major purpose of the Parliamentary Liberal Party as a whole: to sustain the power of a leadership which, in a rough and ready way, skimmed the cream of the administrative talent available in the Liberal ranks in both Houses of Parliament. It was this belief that Administration is the highest form of politics – the greatest legacy of the Peelites to the Liberals – that helped to make the governing hierarchy of the Liberal Party in the age of Gladstone something of a distinct group within, but also apart from, the

Parliamentary Party; a group with its own traditions, its own loyalties, and its own code of disinterested, efficient and highminded service.

The meeting at Willis's rooms, however, and the development of the Parliamentary Liberal Party, is only one side of the story of Liberalism in the 1860s. What is much more important, John Vincent has argued in an important book, is the growth of change – not at the centre – but at the grass roots; the development of new social forces in the country at large which looked to the Parliamentary Liberal Party for leadership and expression. What were these new social forces? There were, Dr Vincent suggests, three: the creation of a cheap daily provincial Press, the growth of militant nonconformity, and the rise of organised labour (**13**).

The rise of a popular Press in the mid-Victorian years was one of the great silent social revolutions of the age. The repeal of the stamp and paper duties between 1855 and 1861 – together with the railway, the telegraph and the steam press – enabled the cheap provincial Press to make a great leap forward in both number of newspapers and circulation, and thus destroy the exclusive metropolitan domination of the 'respectable' newspapers like *The Times*. Moreover, this new provincial Press was dominated mainly by local Liberal politicians, such as the Baines family with the *Leeds Mercury*, the Cowen's *Newcastle Chronicle*, and the Leader family's *Sheffield Independent*. These men used their papers for Liberal – often radical – proselytisation, and helped to build up, therefore, an articulate self-conscious provincial liberalism which became one of the pillars of the new Liberal Party.

Another pillar was militant nonconformity [**doc. 1**]. The nonconformist community as a whole, with the notable exception of the Wesleyans, had always of course traditionally looked towards the old Whig party as the opponents of that exclusive Anglicanism that marked their Tory rivals. That allegiance was now potentially available to the Liberal Party also, as the best instrument through which the nonconformists could realise those special religious, social and educational reforms which would transform the purely legal equality granted to them in 1828 into practical reality. But they were no longer prepared to continue as the Whigs' poor relation; and in the 1860s they were, they believed, in a position to make their weight felt. For they were now a dynamic, militant, wealthy and expanding community – the great Religious Census of 1851 had shown that about half the churchgoing population of the kingdom now belonged to the nonconformist communities. That wealth and those votes, together with their influence, their zeal and their organising ability, they were prepared to place at the disposal of the Liberal Party in return for the fond – but, as it turned out, delusive – expectation that the Parliamentary Party would foster their special interests. Thus began that peculiar love-hate relationship between the Liberal establishment and the nonconformist world which lasted until, in the early twentieth century, the power of organised nonconformity declined, and with it, eventually, the Liberal Party itself (**20**).

As with the nonconformists, so with the new working-class *élite* of trade union leaders and skilled artisans who were prospering with the mid-Victorian boom. Emancipation for them too could be expressed by supporting and voting for the Liberal Party: not only in the sense that, like the nonconformists, they had special interests to achieve – over trade union rights, wages, hours of work – but in a more profound political and psychological way. 'To vote Liberal', as Vincent suggests, 'was closely tied to the growing ability of whole new classes to stand on their own feet' (**13**, p. xiv). Working-class liberalism was thus not entirely, or even mainly, based on simple economic motivation, and the provincial industrial workers were often at one with their masters in their support for the Liberal cause against the forces represented locally by Squire and Parson. Indeed, questions of personal status and subtle pressures *within* a local urban community were as much the determinants of Liberal allegiance generally, as the more overt economic and religious grievances (**110, 113**).

In the 1860s, therefore, the Parliamentary Liberal Party became of major importance in the political life of the country because it established links with these new dynamic forces in the nation at large. The man who saw their importance and carried through this liaison, who used these great religious and social movements to breathe life into the dry bones of the Parliamentary Liberal Party, was W. E. Gladstone. By doing so he was able to assert an almost unquestioned personal ascendancy over them all for the next twenty years, and became, in Magnus's phrase, 'the inspired prophet of the nineteenth-century liberal experiment' (**16**, p. xii).

Yet Gladstone had begun his political life as a vigorous High Churchman and Tory, and it was not until the 1850s, by which time he was the outstanding leader of the Peelites in the House of Commons, that he started seriously to reconsider his early opinions. In 1859 came a decisive moment in his career when, as we have seen, over issues of foreign policy and because he was tired of being out of office, he joined Palmerston's new government as Chancellor of the Exchequer. Gladstone's great free trade budgets of the early 'sixties were decisive in his career. They not only won him the support of the commercial and manufacturing classes in the country, but also established his authority in Parliament and his indispensability to the government (**50**). They also led though, owing to the way in which he stood up to both the Prime Minister and the House of Lords over his Paper Bill, to murmurings on the right-wing of the Liberal bloc: 'The Whigs hate Gladstone', wrote Sir Robert Phillimore in 1860; and one of the greatest of that clan, Lord Clarendon, described the Chancellor as 'an audacious innovator with an insatiable desire of popularity... his ungratified personal vanity makes him wish to subvert the institutions and classes that stand in the way of his ambition'(**16**). Indeed, Gladstone's independent stance in the government made him no more popular in the House than he had been in his Peelite days. Now, however, it mattered less, since, as Gladstone began to observe with increasing satisfaction, a mass opinion was being built up outside the House of Commons which moved gradually but inexorably towards him as its parliamentary spokesman. For the repeal of the paper duties – the 'taxes on knowledge' – not only helped to reinforce a middle-class provincial liberalism based on a cheap press, it helped also to sponsor a working-class liberalism – to educate the country's future masters.

Indeed, the main theme of Gladstone's political life in the 'sixties is his fairly steady move to the left, much to the dismay of the Prime Minister (**45**). What this now meant in practical terms was an increasing respect for and sympathy with the aspirations of the working classes and, to some extent, the nonconformists. And both cause and effect of this was Gladstone's growing awareness of his superb power as a mass orator to move men, as seen in his great tours of the North of England. It was not that he had any real understanding of the life of the working-class audiences he addressed, nor, as he insisted, much to offer them directly that would mitigate the harshness of their lives. But what he could do with his inspiring oratory (which reads so tortuously today) was to raise their status as human beings, to bring them into touch, albeit vicariously, with the wider dramatic political conflicts of the age. He appealed, as Magnus suggests, not to their self-interest but to their self-respect (**16**). By the mid-'sixties Gladstone was convinced that the English workers' attitude, as shown by their fortitude in Lancashire during the cotton famine, their build-up of trade unions and friendly societies, and their support for his new savings banks, was, as he said, 'one of confidence in the law, in parliament, even in the executive government' (14).

The outcome of this new conviction was his famous declaration in May 1865: 'I venture to say that every man who is not presumably incapacitated by some consideration of personal unfitness or of political danger, is morally entitled to come within the pale of the constitution' (15, i). It is true that under the prompting of Palmerston Gladstone did put a more conservative gloss on the words. But the democratic implications were unmistakable, and were drawn increasingly by those working people who saw him more and more as – 'the People's William'. In the general election of that year his fellow-travelling with democracy and dissent lost him his seat at Oxford University; but he stood for South Lancashire. 'At last my friends', he said in a speech at Manchester, 'I am come among you, and I am come among you "unmuzzled" ' ', the famous remark which seems to sum up, politically and psychologically, Gladstone's development in the 'sixties. In the course of the next two years he was able to establish even more closely that favour with the masses which enabled him to emerge, despite Disraeli's tactical victory, as the real hero of 1867 and, in the following year, Prime Minister.

Whence, however, sprang Gladstone's Liberalism? He had, after all, no great sympathy with the more obvious causes of nineteenth-century Liberalism – equality, social improvement, republicanism, anti-clericalism. The first great source was his religion. Gladstone believed fervently that politics was or should be a field of Christian action. One notion that followed from this was Gladstone's conception of 'freedom', which for him was a positive ideal of self-fulfilment and moral development, for nations as well as individuals. How then could a Christian and a Liberal ignore the demand for freedom of a people 'rightly struggling to be free'? In such a situation – whether over Bulgaria in 1876, or Ireland in the 1880s – driven by the creation of what he called a 'virtuous passion', Gladstone threw caution to the winds and was prepared to abandon everything else for the successful pursuance of this great Christian ideal. On such occasions he became incapable of moderation and almost believed – like Cromwell – that God was working through him, and the multitudes who followed where he led. The second source of Gladstone's Liberalism is virtually the corollary of the first. Gladstone was a great 'popular' statesman because he became more and more convinced in the 'seventies and 'eighties of the 'selfishness' of the upper classes and the 'goodness' of the masses. Who, after all, consistently opposed him over Bulgaria and Ireland – and why? 'The burden of his song', wrote a fellow Liberal in 1871, 'is always the deterioration of the Governing Classes in comparison with the poor. He said very solemnly that our Lord's teaching goes very deep in this direction as to the poor being better and wiser than the rich' (**13**, p. 216). By 1880 this had become the semi-mystical belief that a special *rapport* existed between himself and the people, united together against the unwavering hostility of the Victorian Establishment. Nowhere is this feeling expressed more vividly than in his great speech at West Calder during the Midlothian Campaign [**doc. 2**]. It was this extraordinary juxtaposition of alien elements, and especially his passionate moralism, that gave Gladstone his strength and weakness in politics. Everyone admits his dominating personality, his remarkable powers of work, his administrative gifts, his supreme oratorical powers both in the Commons and outside, and his command of popular aspirations. But he was also – perhaps because of these gifts, as A. F. Thompson suggests – a bad party leader and party manager, tactless and awkward with many of his colleagues, and neglecting vital issues both of policy and organisation in order to pursue, ruthlessly and relentlessly, his personal crusades (**17**).

Much of this, however, lay in the future. After the great electoral victory of 1868, the Liberal Party was more popular and more united than it was ever to be again in the nineteenth century, and Gladstone's personal position was assured. His first Government has been called by Ensor 'the greatest ministry of Victoria's reign' (**2**); but its successes were due more to the *élan* that affected the whole party in those early hopeful years, and the topics tackled, than to the outstanding abilities of the ministers as a whole. The Government was very much a 'mixed ministry'; containing Whigs, Peelites and radicals, but with the Whigs predominating. On the other hand, the new 'middle-class' ministers (not all of whom were radicals) controlled internal departments with important legislative responsibilities: Bright at the Board of Trade, Lowe at the Treasury, H. A. Bruce at the Home Office, W. E. Forster in charge of Education, and Cardwell at the War Office.

It was the last three who were mainly responsible for the important, though long overdue, reforms in the field of law, the civil service, trade unionism, education, elections and the army, on which the Government's record is largely based. Gladstone, though in general he approved of what was done, left the details of the Bills to his ministers. He himself was engrossed in the 'pacification' of Ireland, which he believed would be achieved through the passage of three great reforms – in religion, land and education. The passing of the Irish Church Act in 1869, which disendowed and disestablished the Church of Ireland, was a great personal triumph for the Prime Minister, and showed his qualities at their best. But the Irish Land Act of 1870 was largely a failure, and the Irish Universities Bill was defeated in the House of Commons in 1873 and led, though only temporarily, to Gladstone's retirement as premier. By 1873, in fact, the uneasy coalition of forces that had won for the Liberals their remarkable victory in 1868 was split wide apart, and the seeds of disunity and disillusionment were already at work [**doc. 3**]. How had this come about?

Decline

One of the major causes of Liberal disunity was the opposition of the nonconformists to Forster's 1870 Education Act [**doc. 4**]. This Act not only failed to provide that system of free, national and secular education to which the nonconformists were now committed, but seemed to favour the Anglican religious schools by increasing their state grants and allowing them, through the notorious Clause 25, to obtain some measure of rate aid as well. The nonconformists had their own educational 'pressure group' in the form of the National Education League, founded at Birmingham in 1869 by Joseph Chamberlain and a group of local radicals; and as a result of their detestation of the Government's educational policy the activities of the League became more political and more extreme. 'With this knowledge of our opinions', wrote Chamberlain, 'the Government has chosen deliberately to defy us.... This conduct leaves us no alternative.... The great principle of religious equality must be accepted as part of the Programme of any Party which in future seeks our support and alliance. The "Nonconformist Revolt" long threatened has at last begun...'(**26**, i, 137).

By 1873, in fact, a second great stream of discontent with the Liberal Government had come to a head: the Trade Union Revolt had also begun. For in 1871 the Government, following the Report of the Royal Commission on Trade Unions set up in 1867, passed a new Trade Union Act. This gave the unions full legal recognition, but took away from them the right of 'peaceful picketing' by passing a separate Criminal Law Amendment Act which not only made unionists still liable to prosecution under the 1825 Act but, owing to an amendment added by the Lords, made the requirements of that act even stricter. This attitude of the Liberal Government was greeted with bitter resentment by the trade unions – especially after the infamous way in which the law was actually applied in various *causes célèbres* – and prompted great agitation for the repeal of the Amendment Act, led by the recently formed Trades Union Congress (**124**). It was this agitation which, in the words of the Webbs, 'became during the next four years the most significant feature of the Trade Union World' (**123**, p. 283); and as a result the labour movement became not only increasingly antipathetic to official Liberalism, but more politically minded and more independent.

The year 1873 was in fact climacteric in the history of the first Liberal administration. The first great burst of reforms had petered out. The Government was rapidly losing the support of those vital forces – nonconformists, working men and radicals – which had won it the notable victory of 1868, and becoming that 'range of exhausted volcanoes' of Disraeli's brilliant gibe [**doc. 5**]. By the new year Gladstone had reached the decision to dissolve, and he believed that 'Repeal of the Income Tax' was an election cry which would win back public confidence and reunite the party. In addition, the refusal of the Service ministers, Cardwell and Goschen, to accept fully the proposed reduction in their estimates, provided the Prime Minister with 'that perfectly honourable difference of opinion' on the basis of which he could urge the Queen to dissolve. On 24 January 1874 the dissolution of Parliament was announced to a startled country. The National Education League was caught unprepared. The unexpected dissolution was described by the *Nonconformist* as 'a bolt from an unclouded sky which dished the Radicals' (**91**). For the League had expected that the Ministry would last another year, and the sudden dissolution shattered the morale of the nonconformist bloc. How were they to vote when faced with a Liberal candidate? The outcome of the general election of 1874 was an overall majority of fifty for Mr Disraeli, and many League supporters went down to defeat, including Joseph Chamberlain at Sheffield. The trade union movement was better prepared, though in the end they were hardly more successful than the League – only two Labour candidates were returned out of thirteen who stood.

Why then did the Liberal Party lose the election? Much has been made of the 'Nonconformist Revolt'. Francis Adams, the historian of the League, estimated that about twenty seats were lost to the Liberals through nonconformist abstentions at the polls (**19**), but it seems fairly certain that the importance of the League generally as an influence in the Liberal *débâcle* has been exaggerated. Nonconformist voters were, after all, as Professor Hanham has emphasised, concentrated in the under-represented cities of the North and Midlands (**85**); and though there were a large number of seats – thirty-four – where unauthorised Liberals stood owing to party divisions, Arthur Peel, the Liberal Chief Whip, estimated that only thirteen were lost due to those divisions (**91**). For the education issue was only one, and not perhaps the most important issue in the election. 'We have been borne down in a torrent of gin and beer,' said Gladstone in a phrase which has stuck, and the 'brewers revolt' – in opposition to the Licensing Act of 1872 – though its effects have been exaggerated, was an important factor. Even more important was working-class opposition to the Criminal Law Amendment Act. 'The law of conspiracy is their 25th clause,' as Frederic Harrison, the radical, shrewdly said; and some trade unionists probably abstained, following the advice given by their leaders, and some probably voted Conservative. Perhaps the most important reason of all was, quite simply, the swing of the middle-class voter, alarmed by the rise of the working classes, to the Conservative Party, particularly in suburbia, as all sections of political society recognised [**doc. 6**]. And all these factors were worsened for the disunited Liberal Party by the raggedness of its party organisation compared with that of its opponents.

2 Disraeli's Conservative Party

The Second Reform Act

The policy of Sir Robert Peel in trying to provide a more progressive ethos for his party in the early nineteenth century ground to a halt in 1846. By 1865, after twenty years in the wilderness under the leadership of the Earl of Derby in the Lords and, more precariously, Disraeli in the Commons, little had been done to provide the Conservative Party with new supporters, new policies or new enthusiasm (77). What changed the outlook for the party was the death of Palmerston. This produced a more 'fluid' situation after years of torpor, and the possibility therefore of a realignment of political forces from which the Conservatives could benefit. The events of 1866 – the introduction of the Liberal Reform Bill, the Adullamite revolt, the defeat of the Bill – produced just such a situation, and led in June to the establishment of a minority Conservative Government under Derby and Disraeli. The motives that now governed the Conservative leaders, and the tactics that were pursued by Disraeli especially, in the course of the next twelve months down to the passing of the final Act, have been analysed in almost microscopic detail by a group of recent historians (11, 12, 126). As a result, a whole political mythology has been virtually destroyed. It is now clear that Disraeli's attitude during the Reform Crisis was purely opportunist. He neither sought to 'educate his party', nor displayed either firmness or consistency of purpose in his support for 'democracy'. Indeed, during these months Disraeli had only one major aim: to destroy Gladstone's leadership over a united Liberal Party, and, by seizing the initiative in reform himself and promoting a Reform Bill, to consolidate his own leadership of the Conservative Party. The latter point is particularly important in view of Disraeli's tenuous hold over the party in the Commons in the 1850s. For, as Maurice Cowling has argued, Disraeli's brilliant tactical success in 1867 was not just a victory over Gladstone and the Liberals; it was as much a personal victory within his own party. It meant 'that Derby and Disraeli were going to run the

Conservative Party, not Cranborne and Peel, and that those elements in the party which wanted to get rid of Disraeli would have to destroy the party in the process' (**12**, p. 164). Why did the party follow Disraeli? Not only, suggests Mr Cowling, for party advantage, but because the final Act itself had 'conservative' as well as 'democratic' implications (**12**). It is the 'conservative' aspect of the Second Reform Act that is of fundamental importance in considering the position of the Conservative Party after 1867.

To many contemporaries, both of the Left and the Right, the Second Reform Act seemed to be an essentially democratic measure which gave effective political power to the working class. Superficially this appeared to be true. Nearly a million new voters were added to the electoral list, and the increase was widest in the great cities where working-class voters now became a majority. But the position in the counties was very different, and does much to justify Mr Cowling's remark that Disraeli 'was prepared to let Radicals have their way in the boroughs, so long as he had his to some extent in the counties' (**12**, p. 233). For in the counties the vote was given only to the twelve-pound householders, a deferential group, which meant that the number of voters rose only from 540,000 to 790,000 – an increase of only 40 per cent compared with a 134 per cent increase in the boroughs. In addition, since in county areas the rural districts were strongly reinforced by boundary changes which deliberately lopped off suburban areas and added them to the boroughs, conditions there were not very much different after 1867. In the counties, therefore, the old order continued almost undisturbed, and they remained the chief stronghold of the Conservative Party which, in the later nineteenth century, regularly won in them twice as many seats as its opponents (**85**).

In any case the question of the franchise, from a long-term point of view, was not the most important aspect of the Reform Act. Much more significant was what Bright called 'the very soul of the question of reform' – the problem of redistribution. Here, the 'conservative' nature of the Bill was even more clearly evident. For in England only forty-five seats were redistributed in 1867, and twenty-five of these went to the counties to enlarge an already conservative franchise; while the four greatest provincial cities – Manchester, Birmingham, Leeds and Liverpool – were fobbed off with an extra member, bringing their representation up to only three members each. This lack of a fundamental redistribution of seats meant that not only were Liberal votes piled up and wasted in the great centres of population, whereas Conservative votes were more evenly distributed throughout the country, but that many of the old anomalies remained. After 1867 there were still more than seventy boroughs with a population of less than 10,000 voters, and the boroughs as a whole were still considerably over-represented. Hence many of the corrupt electoral habits of a previous political era were carried over into the post-Reform period; and, despite the Ballot Act of 1872, corruption, bribery and deference remained important features of the new electoral system for at least another generation.

What all this meant was that the Second Reform Act did not mark that fundamental break in English political life which its supporters had expected and its enemies dreaded. This did not come about until the 1880s. The year 1867 did not inaugurate an age of Democracy; did not in fact give the working classes direct political power; no workingman, for example, was to be returned at the general election of 1868 [**doc. 7**]. What it did was not to revolutionise the direction of government, but to produce a major transformation in the relationship of the Electorate and Government. In the light of these considerations, the Act of 1867 offered to the Conservative Party positive advantages both of policy and electoral strategy. Whether these advantages would be seized, and how they would be used, depended very much on the relationship between Disraeli, the Parliamentary Party and the new electorate.

Disraelian Conservatism

Disraeli became Prime Minister in 1868 after Derby's retirement, a direct consequence of his political triumph in the preceding year [**doc. 8**]. But though he had now reached the top of the greasy pole (in his own famous phrase) his position as Conservative leader was by no means completely assured (**79**). His support for 'democracy' in 1867 had incurred the bitter opposition and distrust of the right wing of the party led by its intellectual mentor, Robert Cecil, now Marquis of Salisbury. And, as Salisbury argued with virulent conviction, the electoral rout that soon followed was not only a sufficient condemnation of Disraeli's leadership, but a direct consequence of his 'grave political insincerity' (**57**). Nor was the opposition solely reactionary and aristocratic. Conservative reformers like Cross and Sandon were also sceptical about Disraeli's effectiveness as a leader, a mood which was enhanced in many sections of the party by his refusal to take office in 1873. Moreover, the very magnitude of the Liberals' victory and the reasonableness of many of their

13

reform proposals, was bound to make effective opposition difficult for any Conservative leader. But Disraeli suffered further from the fact that his leadership was purely personal: he was not associated with any of the sections of the Conservative Party nor, unlike the Liberal leader, was he able to draw upon any great reserves of influence in the nation at large. The Conservatives, as Feuchtwanger suggests, were never Disraeli's party as the Liberals were Gladstone's (**99**, p. 28). His policy up to 1874, therefore, aimed at ensuring his own political survival by exercising his rightful authority without upsetting too many Tory susceptibilities – and looking towards the future. This meant temporising over Liberal reforms, and then cashing in on the growing Liberal disunity and unpopularity they helped to produce. At the same time Disraeli outlined a general Conservative programme in his public speeches in 1872 which could appeal to all sections of the community; and, above all, he concentrated on building up a superior party organisation.

It was these tactics that seemed to pay off in the General Election of 1874, when the Conservatives made important gains in the boroughs and won an overall majority of fifty. It was this electoral victory – the first Conservative one since 1841 – rather than the events of 1867–68, which really made Disraeli master of the Conservative Party. 'After thirty years of scorn and sullenness', as he observed of the Tory aristocracy, 'they have melted before time and events' (**55**). This new *rapprochement*, and indeed the new forces affecting Conservatism, were seen when Disraeli formed his Government. Inevitably, given the Prime Minister's predilection for the aristocracy, the Cabinet contained six peers, including Salisbury who thus re-entered the fold. But of much greater significance was the group of commoners, mainly middle-class men, who then or soon afterwards entered the Government: R. A. Cross, a pillar of Lancashire Conservatism, who had never before held office, as Home Secretary; Lord Sandon, a member for Liverpool, in charge of education; Sclater-Booth at the Local Government Board; and W. H. Smith, first at the Admiralty and then at the Treasury. Thus the Government was not only a strong one in its own right, it also represented all the important sections of the party. It was this that helped to keep the Conservatives steadily together for the next six years.

The task that faced the Conservative Party in power, as it had faced it since 1867, was how to win and maintain support among the new voters created by the Second Reform Act without antagonising its traditional supporters, and this depended mainly on the

Party's programme. What in fact was to be the basis of Disraelian Conservatism? The fundamental task of the Conservative Party, Disraeli had written earlier, was 'to uphold the aristocratic settlement of the country', and many writers have seen this aim as the one thread of consistency that runs through all Disraeli's ideas and policies from first to last (58). This was more than just the product of his romantic view of English history and society. For Disraeli, Robert Blake suggests, the 'aristocratic settlement' stood not only for that traditional order and stability – based on 'natural' leadership and rooted in common interests and mutual respect – that he saw epitomised in the rural society of his own county of Buckinghamshire, but for individual freedom (55, pp. 278–82). These principles were the exact antithesis of what he conceived to be the typical evils of the age: Whig cosmopolitanism, the mercenary spirit of the manufacturing classes and the centralising tendencies of the Benthamite radicals. Since these forces were the enemies also of the working classes, we have here the intellectual raw material of so-called 'Tory Democracy'. But to this traditional Conservatism based on 'the maintenance of our institutions' Disraeli added, in his great speech at the Crystal Palace in June 1872, two new principles: 'the preservation of our Empire and the improvement of the condition of the people', the latter point having already been developed in his famous *sanitas sanitatum* speech at Manchester a few months previously [**doc. 9**].

It would, however, be an exaggeration as far as the first principle is concerned to imagine that Disraeli was here offering an ideology of Imperialism to the Conservative Party, at least in the sense of support for a deliberate policy of colonial expansion and taking up 'the white man's burden'. Disraeli's imperialism was more limited, at once emotional and old-fashioned: it was not (as Shannon suggests) 'prophetic of a large new future'(7). He had no interest in colonial affairs as such, though he was fascinated by India and concerned for her security, as his Near Eastern policy and the proclamation of Queen Victoria as Empress of India reveals. He was content to leave the details of local administration and policy to the men on the spot – disastrously as it turned out on the North-West Frontier of India and in South Africa. But he did have a vision of the Empire as a buttress to British military and foreign policy, 'a centralised military empire backing up the strength of Great Britain in her role as a world power and providing both resources and armies beyond the control of Parliament' (71). This was a view which had already been adumbrated by Disraeli in speeches in

1866, and in action through the Abyssinian expedition of 1868. His purpose then, so it has been argued, was to stiffen the will to rule of the English upper classes, and at the same time, during these years of political crisis, damp down class conflicts by the pursuit of 'national' objectives (**72**).

Disraeli's second principle has been seized upon by Conservative apologists as well as historians and political writers, both then and since, who have argued that the Conservative Party under the inspiration of Disraeli adopted a clear consistent programme of social reform in order to win the support of the newly enfranchised working classes, and thus produce that union of the upper classes and the masses that would inaugurate 'Tory Democracy'. 'Disraeli discerned', in the famous comment of *The Times*, 'the Conservative workingman as the sculptor perceives the angel imprisoned in the block of marble'.

But just as the traditional role of Disraeli in the Reform crisis of 1866–67 has come under heavy attack, so too has his role as a social reformer – notably by Dr Paul Smith (**56**). What Dr Smith has shown by a detailed examination of the actual ideas and legislation of the Conservative Party in the field of social policy between 1866 and 1880 is how little of real substance there is in the popular view of Disraeli as an apostle of social reform. It is true that he did something to orient his party in favour of 'the elevation of the condition of the People' in his speeches in 1872, in order to capture the working-class vote. But in practice all that Disraeli provided for his party were the verbal trappings of reform; after 1874 the choice of topics for legislative action and their detailed execution was left to middle-class outsiders such as R. A. Cross – 'the workhorse of the administration'. This was partly because Disraeli was over seventy when he achieved real power and, inevitably, lacked the energy of a Peel or a Gladstone; but it was also because, as Cross saw clearly but regretfully, Disraeli lacked that interest in, or grasp of, administrative detail so essential for the social reformer [**doc. 10**]. And even such interest as Disraeli possessed in what a Conservative back-bencher called 'suet-pudding legislation', waned rapidly after 1876 in favour of ideas more in harmony with his flamboyant imagination: *imperium et libertas* instead of *sanitas sanitatum*. Nor is it easy to see anything approaching a Conservative 'programme' of social reform during this period. 'Empiricism tempered by prejudice', in Dr Smith's phrase, remained the basis of the party's approach to social problems, and such problems were taken up and dealt with – or dropped – as and when political exigencies or public pressures demanded (**56**). Nevertheless, it would be unfair not to pay tribute to what was accomplished by Cross, Sandon and Sclater-Booth in the fields of education, housing, public health and labour legislation, in particular, during the three great years 1874 to 1876. In that period the Conservatives passed eleven major Acts. 'It was', concludes Dr Smith, 'a considerable performance'; but, he adds, 'it was of rather mixed quality . . . if only the Licensing Act was a mistake, only the settlement of the labour laws was a triumph, and the remaining measures were cautious, limited, and even weak' (**56**, p. 202). Why was this? The answer to that question tells us much about the Conservative Party and the pressures to which it was subject in the 1870s.

For though, as Disraeli and the more clear-headed members of the Government realised, the Conservative Party had now to appeal more directly to the working-class electorate – and social reform could be conceived as one means towards that end – they could not afford to alienate their traditional supporters in the country or in the Commons. And the plain fact about the Conservative Party in the 1870s was that, despite the growing number of industrialists in its ranks and the appointment of a bookseller to the Cabinet, it was still primarily the party of the country gentry. Two hundred out of 350 Conservative M.P.s returned in 1874 were associated with the landed interest; and, unlike their Liberal opposite numbers, they were largely unrestrained by any systematic outside pressure from, for example, organisations like the National Education League. It was their ethos therefore that dominated the party, and, inevitably, the country gentry were often unsympathetic to the new tensions and problems that faced the party leadership. What often inhibited a bold Conservative social policy, therefore, were the ineluctable pressures of prejudice and vested interest within the party: suspicion of centralisation, devotion to the dogmas of *laisser faire* and, above all, blind opposition to anything – votes for labourers, higher rates, elected schoolboards, trade unions – that would upset the established order in the English shires. Even the reformers largely accepted these presuppositions. Lord Sandon's purpose in his Education Act of 1876 was, *inter alia*, to free the countryside from school boards – 'the favourite platforms of the Dissenting preacher and the local agitator' (**56**, p. 246). In the end, therefore, it was only the mildness and limited nature of the Government's social reforms that made them palatable to the country gentry.

But there was another, more profound, reason for the limitations of Conservative social policy. For the Second Reform Act had a paradoxical effect. If, on the one hand, it created a mass working-class electorate that could be won for the Conservative Party, it also helped, by its invocation of democracy, to create those fears and apprehensions among the middle classes that would slowly drive them away from the Liberal Party. After 1867 the Conservative Party became increasingly attractive to an urban bourgeoisie whose members were more and more appalled by Gladstonian 'energy' and the rise of the working class in social and political power; and the Conservative leadership was bound to attune its policy accordingly. 'We came in', said Disraeli after the 1874 election, 'on the principle of not harassing the country.' The Conservatives were compelled, therefore, during this period to appeal more and more to the middle, rather than the working, class, especially as they needed their support as leaders in the new borough conservative associations. This meant that though social legislation could be used to win over the workers, it must not be so radical as to frighten away the middle class; its distinctly 'class' nature must be toned down. Nor was it only middle-class voters that Disraeli had to worry about: the great forces of industrial and commercial wealth – rapidly coalescing with the older landed interest in the Conservative Party – had also to be conciliated. It is this that helps to explain why the Government was so often willing to yield – unless browbeaten by the righteous wrath of a Samuel Plimsoll – to the vested interests of mineowners, brewers and shipowners.

Here we have the dilemma of the Conservative Party in the 1870s and indeed later. How could it provide policies which would appeal to the working classes without frightening away the middle classes? The answer provided by Disraeli after 1876 was to stress 'national' rather than 'class' policies; policies that high-lighted not the special class interests of the workers, but rather what they had in common with the rest of the community. As he said, in a famous comment, 'I have always considered that the Tory party was the national party of England' (**69**). This meant an emphasis on the mutual interests of the working classes and the classes above them, led by their 'natural' leaders in the Conservative Party, in supporting the country's institutions – Monarchy, Church, Aristocracy – as outlined in the Prime Minister's earlier speeches. It also meant, more importantly, a vigorous foreign and imperial policy. This can be seen in Disraeli's purchase of the Suez Canal shares, his belligerent attitude towards Russia in 1878, and his 'forward' policies in Afghanistan and South Africa in 1879, though these at least were initiated by the men on the spot, Lord Lytton, the Viceroy of India, and Sir Bartle Frere, High Commissioner at the Cape. But these policies were not just the result of the Prime Minister's own interests and prejudices and misapprehensions. They were also, in a sense, an attempt to escape from the internal contradictions of Conservative domestic policy in the 'seventies by a brilliant display abroad. Unhappily for Disraeli, it was this strategy that collapsed in ruins at the General Election of 1880.

In that election the Conservative Party lost more than 100 seats, and all the gains made in 1874 were wiped out. They lost most heavily in the large boroughs where, out of 114 seats, they now had only twenty-four; though on the other hand they did well in the City of London and London suburbia. They also lost twenty-seven county seats, and were practically wiped out in Wales and Scotland. In the end, the Liberals gained an overall majority of about fifty, and the swing to them would probably have been even stronger if the fifty-six uncontested. seats had been fought. The Conservative Party seemed, therefore, to be back to where it was in 1868. 'The downfall of Beaconsfieldism',* said Gladstone, 'is like the vanishing of some vast magnificent castle in an Italian romance' (15, vol. 2, p. 223). Curiously, Disraeli himself was never more popular than in this hour of defeat. Supported after his resignation as Prime Minister by a unanimous and enthusiastic vote of confidence, he decided to carry on as party leader, determined to act, as he said in a letter to Lord Lytton, 'as if I were still young and vigorous, and take all steps in my power to sustain the spirit and restore the discipline of the Tory Party' (55, p. 721). With this typically jaunty courage the old statesman carried on for another year until his death in April 1881.

Why then did the Conservatives lose the General Election of 1880 (103)? There were, in the first place, a number of electoral factors which put the Liberals in a stronger position from the start. The timing of the election (as with Gladstone in 1874) was unexpected and unfavourable to the Conservatives. No real reply was made by Disraeli to the attack on 'Beaconsfieldism' proclaimed so passionately by Gladstone in the Midlothian Campaign, and in any case the major Conservative spokesmen during the campaign – owing to the convention by which peers did not participate – were easily outgunned by the Liberals [**doc. 11**]. Furthermore, the Con-

---

* Disraeli had been created Earl of Beaconsfield in 1876. He is referred to throughout by his family name.

servative Party machine had been allowed to run down, especially after the resignation in 1877 of J. A. Gorst, its real creator and the one true Tory Democrat in the party (**99**, ch. 6). Nor, surprisingly, did the Conservatives make much of their record in social reform during the campaign – another indication perhaps of its limited role. Clearly, it was not considered a trump card as far as the working-class voter was concerned; or at least not effective enough to offset the more immediate impact of industrial depression.

It is in fact the depression that has generally been regarded as the major factor in causing the Conservative defeat. Disraeli himself said: 'Hard Times, as far as I can 'collect, has been our foe, and certainly the alleged cause of our downfall' (**55**, p. 719). And the effects of depression were unmistakable. Real wages fell by 5 per cent during 1873–79: the average level of unemployment (as revealed by trade union statistics) rose from 1 or 2 per cent in 1871–74 to 6·8 per cent in 1878, and then rose to 11·4 per cent in 1879, a year of real distress among many sections of the working class. For the farmers too 1879 was a bad year. All that the Government did for them, however – apart from one unsatisfactory Act to provide compensation for improvements – was to appoint the Richmond Commission to investigate the causes of agricultural depression. It was this negative attitude that led to the growth of the Farmers' Alliance, an independent farmers' movement which put up its own candidates at the election and thus helped to produce the slump in Conservative votes in the counties (**85**). Of course, as Disraeli insisted, the coming of depression was bad luck for the Conservative Party, since it could not reasonably be regarded as directly responsible for its onset. But it was undoubtedly true that the Government did little to cope with its consequences. Indeed how could it? It had no more notion of what to do than its opponents – or its successors in the 1920s; nor did it believe that there was much that could be done. Protection was ruled out by Disraeli as a cure for the country's economic ills on political grounds – it would be electoral suicide; the only thing to do, therefore, as W. H. Smith suggested, was, resignedly, to await the return of a more favourable economic cycle. The Conservatives, however, not unfairly, were bound to be blamed for the effects of the Depression; just as Disraeli was blamed by Gladstone for the iniquitous effects of his foreign and imperial policy.

The election of 1880 does much to illuminate the nature of Disraelian Conservatism. It is true, of course, that the Conservative Party, mainly under Disraeli's inspiration, did make a real attempt to enlarge the electoral basis of its strength, and thus provided, in Dr Smith's words, 'a classic case of successful adaptation to a changing environment' (56). This is indicated, to some extent, by the fact that, despite losing two elections, the Conservatives were increasing their votes in industrial seats during the whole period 1868–80; and even in 1880 their proportion of the poll rose by 7 per cent in large constituencies. But, as we have already seen, the social policy of the Conservatives was not really well adapted to the purpose of winning over the working-class voters; electorally, as the verdict of 1880 seemed to show, it was almost irrelevant, and seems to have done little to wean the workers away from the Liberal Party. Indeed, the Government's trade union legislation – by restoring the right of peaceful picketing – helped to heal the one great breach between organised labour and official Liberalism, and therefore probably precipitated the return of the trade union voter to the Liberal Party. The policy of the Conservative Party, said Disraeli after his resignation in 1880, 'is to maintain the Empire and preserve the Constitution' (55, p. 721). Social reform was now conspicuous by its absence from the great triumvirate of Conservative aims that he had formerly proclaimed in 1872; and indeed Imperialism and the preservation of the *status quo* were to be the Disraelian themes that emerged most distinctly in the Conservative Party of the later nineteenth century.

Part Two: The Struggle

3 Party Organisation

Political parties, if they are to win elections, require not only policies but organisation. Before 1867, however, with a small electorate
the problem was not so urgent, and party organisation was primi-
tive, makeshift and erratic, springing into life only when a general
election was pending. The central organisation of the parties in the
'sixties was normally in the hands of the Whips, whose main task,
apart from their parliamentary duties, was to raise money for the
election fund and obtain candidates, functions they normally per-
formed under the benevolent but aloof authority of the Party Leader. The only practical help the Whips obtained were from the services, part-time and generally unofficial, of an election or party
agent, together with the help of an occasional interested party notable. Nationally, in the counties and boroughs, party affairs were in
the hands of virtually self-appointed and self-perpetuating committees of local party bigwigs, who ran the constituency with the help
of a registration agent for day-to-day business and advice and, at
election times, a paid election agent [doc. 12]. The links between
the central and local party organisers were inevitably very tenuous,
and were conducted mainly through the great London political
clubs: the Carlton (Conservative) founded in 1832, and the Reform
(Liberal) 1836.

The Second Reform Act of 1867 had a decisive effect on the development of party organisation. Both parties now had to win the
votes of a much wider – mainly working-class – electorate, especially in the large boroughs; and the new and often taxing problems
that this posed for the party managers can be seen exemplified in
the correspondence of Glyn and Brand, the Liberal Whips, at the
election of 1868. 'The old lines of a general election do not serve us
now', Glyn wrote to Gladstone, 'all is new and changed and ... I
fear I must say in some respects dark' (92). The period between
1867 and 1886 was essentially a transitional period in party organisation. New and more efficient machinery was created to cope
with the problems of a mass electorate, and active party membership began to become a reality; but all this existed side by side

with the antediluvian methods and ideas of a bygone political age. Two major developments in fact took place. First, organisation at the centre became more professional and more formalised, and both Conservatives and Liberals established a central party office in London [**doc. 13**]. Second, local party organisations were set up throughout the country, concentrated mainly in the large boroughs, and these eventually coalesced to form national organisations – the Conservative National Union (1867) and the National Liberal Federation (1877). Linked with these were their fellow-travelling organisations and pressure groups; the powerful Liberal Liberation Society, for example, and, in the 'eighties, the tamer Conservative Primrose, and Fair Trade, Leagues.

The two great national organisations, however, though of major importance as propaganda and 'ginger' groups for the Conservative and Liberal Parties, did pose a frightening problem for the party leaders: might they not use their broad-based power to dictate to the parliamentary parties? Thus the problem of the relationship between the parliamentary parties, on the one hand, and the Conservative National Union and Liberal Federation, on the other, proved to be one of the great themes in the history of party organisation in the later nineteenth century. But the fear of 'caucus control' – dictation to Parliament by outside irresponsible bodies – which so worried political commentators in the 'seventies and 'eighties, and was later given classic expression in Ostrogorski's great book, proved in the end to be an illusion (**88**). By the turn of the century the leaders of both parties had, in McKenzie's phrase, 'shackled the monster they had created', and the pattern of party organisation then established persisted, with minor modifications, well into the twentieth century (**89**).

The Conservative Party

For the Conservative Party, lacking those unofficial lines of communication between party and people which were established by the Liberals in the 1860s, efficient national organisation was an absolute necessity. But just as the problems of Conservative 'policy' after the passing of the Second Reform Act had aroused tensions and conflicts within the party, so too did the problems of organisation. Should it be 'popular' organisation, appealing directly to and involving the middle and working classes; or should it be 'authoritarian', directed from above by the traditional hierarchy of Party Leader, aristocratic Whips and part-time aides? The conflict between these two conceptions had arisen as early as 1867 at the formation of the Conservative National Union. It soon affected Disraeli's first major step in improving central party organisation – the establishment of the Conservative Central Office in 1870 and the appointment of J. A. Gorst as party agent.

Gorst, a clear-headed and vigorous administrator, aimed primarily at improving Conservative organisation in the large boroughs, which meant appealing directly to the working class. During the next few years he was extraordinarily successful. By the end of 1873 Gorst was able to report to Disraeli that sixty-nine new Conservative Associations had been founded, and that more than 400 Associations were in existence throughout the country, including thirty-three in the forty-nine largest boroughs. It was here, in the larger boroughs, that the influence of the Central Office was strongest; the smaller boroughs and, even more, the counties, were willy-nilly allowed to go their own way. By the time of the General Election in 1874 a Conservative candidate had been found for every reasonable constituency, and Gorst's efforts seemed to be rewarded by the Conservative victory at the polls (**99**, ch. 5).

The other significant development in Conservative Party organisation during this period was the foundation of the National Union in 1867. Here too the initiative came, not, as with the National Liberal Federation, from below, but from above. 'The National Union was organised', said Henry Raikes, one of its founders, 'rather as a handmaid to the party, than to usurp the functions of party leadership' (**90**, p. 259). The inaugural meeting of the Union on 12 November 1867 assembled sixty-seven delegates from fifty-five cities: Gorst took the chair in the absence of a peer! But despite the Union's ostensible aim of winning over the working class, the emphasis in electing officers was on 'men of influence and prestige', not working men, an illuminating illustration of the ambivalent attitude of the Conservative Party in the post-Reform epoch. Indeed, though the Union did good work in issuing pamphlets etc., by the election of 1868 it was practically moribund as an independent organisation – a clear reflection of its lack of consistent purpose and the absence of outstanding party leaders from its councils. When, in 1871, Gorst became its Secretary and transferred its headquarters to his own offices as Party Agent in Parliament Street, the National Union became in practice what it had always really been in theory, the propaganda arm of the Conservative Central Office.

The foundation of the National Union in 1867 and the Central

Office in 1870 were, as Feuchtwanger says, 'the most important permanent legacy of the period' (**99**, p. xiii). But they produced no fundamental change in the structure of the party, and were largely ignored or opposed by the traditionalists. Hence the same old battles were fought after 1874 as before. For, foolishly, the party leaders not only allowed the machine which had been carefully built up in the previous four years to run down, but encouraged the central control of the party organisation to pass from Gorst (whose engagement as party agent officially ended in 1874) back to the Whips – the representatives of the aristocratic element in the party. Gorst, who had in any case become a member of Parliament in 1875 and was anxious to carve out a political career for himself, resigned in disgust in 1877 after warning Disraeli of the dangers now facing the party (**99**, pp. 137–8). Panic-stricken by the electoral disaster of 1880, the party managers hastily turned back to Gorst who was re-engaged as party agent, and a new permanent Central Committee, ostensibly representing all sections of the party, was set up to supervise organisation [**doc. 14**]. Yet the old antagonisms between the cantankerous party agent and the party managers soon cropped up again. Outwardly, these concerned control of finance, demarcation of responsibility, and similar problems; but Gorst saw them, more fundamentally, as an attempt by the Conservative 'old gang' to re-establish control, a claim which was given additional weight by the similar unhappy experience of his successor, G. C. T. Bartley, who became party agent in 1882 [**doc. 15**]. Disillusioned, Bartley too resigned – as did Winn, the Chief Whip – in 1885. Their replacement by Capt. Middleton as party agent and Akers-Douglas as Chief Whip, together with the fact that the electoral legislation of 1883–85 had revolutionised the conditions of political life, began something of a new era in the central organisation of the Conservative Party (**89**).

Before this could be achieved, one final problem had to be settled: the revival of the National Union under the dynamic leadership of Lord Randolph Churchill. Since 1880 Lord Randolph had built up a brilliant reputation as leader of the 'Fourth Party' in the House of Commons; a minuscule group which consisted, apart from himself, of his friends J. A. Gorst, Drummond Wolff and A. J. Balfour (**61**, ch. 3). Churchill's main task, and one which he carried out with extraordinary skill and panache, was to harass and hold up to ridicule the Liberal Government in the House of Commons, and especially its aged leader, particularly over Ireland and 'the Bradlaugh Case'. His subsidiary aim was to attack the pusillanimous spirit displayed by his own leader in the House, Sir Stafford Northcote, and the absurd arrangement by which, since Disraeli's death in 1881, he had shared power with Lord Salisbury in the Upper House. In many ways, therefore, as his support for the independent leadership of Lord Salisbury indicates, Lord Randolph was advocating a more pugnacious brand of traditional Toryism, rather than 'Tory Democracy', the name with which his ideas are usually branded (**74**). But what really moved him in the early 'eighties was not policy, which meant little to him – his politics were, as R. R. James suggests, 'mainly intuitive' – but personal ambition and, it must be said, delight in battle for its own sake (**61**). What he wanted to do after 1882 was to lever himself into the front rank of the Conservative Party by sheer effrontery and oratorical brilliance; and in the National Union the instrument for his purposes lay at hand. He set out, therefore, to capture it.

The National Union in 1883 was in many ways admirably adapted for Churchill's plans. It had in the 1870s quietly toed the central party line; but now, with nearly 500 Associations affiliated to it, it could be said to represent the real voice of the Conservative Party, and many ordinary Conservatives, appalled by the electoral disaster of 1880, and impressed by the evident success of the National Liberal Federation, were intensely worried by the weaknesses of official Conservatism, and were crying out for full-blooded leadership. It was their hopes and fears that Churchill used, and became spokesman for. Moreover, the unwieldy constitution of the Union could easily be manipulated by a determined 'caucus' of Lord Randolph and his friends; and here the support of Gorst, with his mastery of party organisation, was absolutely priceless. In 1883 the young aristocratic crusader made his bid to capture the Union. He was not completely successful; but he did well enough to become chairman and obtain a small but decisive 'Churchillian' majority on the Council. He then threw down his challenge to Northcote and Salisbury by demanding that real power be given to the National Union; that, in the words of the 1883 Conference resolution, the Union 'secure its legitimate influence in the party organisation'. Thus began that behind-the-scenes struggle between Lord Randolph Churchill and Lord Salisbury which posed yet again the fundamental problem: should the Conservative Party be a 'popular' or an 'authoritarian' organisation? A long period of conflict, negotiation, recrimination and misunderstanding now followed, in which Lord Randolph resigned as chairman, was reinstated in triumph at the Sheffield Conference of the National Union in July 1884, but then, unexpectedly, came to terms with Lord Salisbury. By their agreement, Lord Randolph recognised Lord Salisbury as party leader, and entered the fold himself as a member of the upper party hierarchy; he resigned as Union Chairman and was replaced by Hicks-Beach, but the old Central Committee was then dissolved.

This was really a victory for Lord Salisbury and the official leadership of the Conservative Party. For whereas Lord Randolph regarded the National Union merely as a ladder for his ambition which, once used, could easily be discarded, both Salisbury and Northcote were adamant in their refusal to give up their essential control of the party, and, given their firmness, Churchill was bound to lose. He stood for no new ideas or principles, no new social or economic group in the politics of the 'eighties; the alternative Churchill presented to the Conservative Party was, as Salisbury probably realised, a sham alternative (**62, 74**). In any case, it was not new ideas that the Conservative Party was hankering after during this period; nor were the rank and file in the National Union really protesting against central leadership as such: it was weak leadership they objected to, and Lord Salisbury was soon to give them the strong and effective leadership they demanded. It was, therefore, the anguish of defeat, and not any fundamental change in party ethos, that gave Lord Randolph his brief period of success as a 'popular' politician. As for the National Union it was, in Sir Winston Churchill's phrase, 'peacefully laid to rest' by Michael Hicks-Beach (**60**). Unhappily for Lord Randolph, by throwing away the prop which had brought him to power, he placed himself at the mercy of his former rivals, and thus prepared the way for his later dramatic downfall (**96**).

The Liberal Party

Like the Conservatives the Liberals also established a Central (Registration) Association during this period; but on the whole, partly due to the nature of the Liberal Party, partly due to the lack of anyone like Gorst, it was controlled almost completely by the Whips. Brand and Glyn, Chief Whips between 1857 and 1873, did good work in building up contact between the central organisation and the local Liberal Associations in the immediate post-Reform period. But the fact that there was no great change in either the machinery or the personnel of the Liberal Central Office was relatively unimportant, since the real changes in party organisation came not from above but from below: it was the changes at the grass-roots that were of major importance. Here – as with the campaign for secular education – Birmingham again provided the driving force and example by developing a new and, as some thought, sinister form of organisation – the Caucus.

The Birmingham Liberal Association had been founded in 1865, and from the start differed from the older type of oligarchic association by being open to anyone in the city. It was soon re-modelled by its secretary, William Harris, on a popular but strongly centralised basis, ranging from the elected ward committee at the bottom, through the Central Committee of 600, which nominated parliamentary candidates, to the Central Executive, and the 'Council of Ten' at the top, the brains and will of the whole organisation. In origin, however, the Caucus, as it was dubbed by Disraeli, was neither as original, nor as much the result of malevolent calculation as Ostrogorski made out in his classical study (**88**). What was new about the Caucus of 1867 was not so much its underlying ideas or its methods – since the working class and the middle class in Birmingham had been cooperating mutually in reform politics since the 1830s – but the formalisation of its machinery and its adaptation to an enlarged electorate, an electorate which accepted, naturally, the tutelage of the middle class. Indeed, as T. R. Tholfsen argues convincingly, the Caucus was related directly to the ethos of the Birmingham community, and emerged slowly and naturally out of the rich soil of its economic, social and religious life (**94**). The effectiveness of this new organisation was seen when all three Liberals were returned at the election of 1868 despite the fact that the Second Reform Act had given each elector only two votes; and – especially owing to the work of Francis Schnadhorst who succeeded William Harris in 1873 – the Liberals easily won the School Board and Council elections in the same year. In 1874 the Association's three candidates were returned unopposed at the general election (**93**). The Liberal Party was now supreme in Birmingham, sustained by the power of radical nonconformity.

The defeat of 1874 gave a considerable stimulus to the establishment of 'popular' Liberal Associations in many other great cities, such as Leeds, Sheffield, Bradford, Newcastle; and though they differed from the Birmingham Association in particulars, the Birmingham radicals, as Professor Hanham says, 'supplied the associations with both an ideology and an organisational model' (**85**, p. 133). As yet, however, there was no unified organisation or policy for them all: this Joseph Chamberlain and his radical associates set out to provide. By the mid 'seventies in fact Chamberlain was tiring of the education issue alone as a spearhead of radical attack. 'I don't think the League will do,' he told Dilke in 1873 when he was already thinking in terms of a reconstructed Liberal Party with a wide reform programme and new leaders (**31**). His return, unopposed, as one of the members for Birmingham in 1876, by which time Lord Hartington had succeeded Gladstone as Liberal Leader, only confirmed his disillusionment with official Liberalism. When, therefore, in the same year William Harris proposed to Chamberlain a national radical organisation linking all the 'pressure' groups – National Education League, Liberation Society etc. – and based on the Liberal Associations, he took up the idea enthusiastically, insisting only that it be based on Birmingham, and notices were sent to all associations organised on a 'popular' basis to send delegates to a national conference to be held at Birmingham on 31 May 1877.

The year 1876 was important, however, for another reason. It was the year when Gladstone re-emerged from retirement to become one of the leaders of the Bulgarian Agitation directed against Disraeli's Eastern policy. The Agitation – strongly supported by radicals and nonconformists – thus provided the background, though not as Ostrogorski believed the original stimulus, for the foundation of the National Liberal Federation. That, as Professor Herrick has argued, was provided by the National Education League which, after it was wound up in the spring of 1877, bequeathed its pattern of organisation, its sectarian passion and much of its personnel to the new organisation (**95**).

We are just going to issue the League's dissolution circular [wrote Chamberlain to John Morley in February 1877], announcing at the same time the formation of a Federation of Liberal Associations with hq at Birmingham and the League Officers as chief cooks. I think this may become a very powerful organisation and proportionately detested by all Whips and Whigs (**26**, i, 258).

The inaugural meeting took place at Birmingham as planned. There, with Chamberlain acting as President and his henchman, Jesse Collings, as Secretary, a constitution and statement of policy was drawn up for the new National Liberal Federation. The meeting was not a complete success. Only about half of the hundred or so delegates agreed to join, owing to fears for their local autonomy, and of the 'pressure' groups, only the National Education League, as we have seen, agreed to commit suicide to please Mr Chamberlain. The Federation, however, held its first meeting at Birmingham on 22 July 1877. Joseph Chamberlain was elected President; William Harris, Chairman; Jesse Collings, Hon. Secretary, and Francis Schnadhorst, paid Secretary; three subcommittees were set up and a central office in Birmingham [**doc. 18**]. By 1879 the new Secretary's organising genius had brought in over 100 Liberal Associations, though nearly all were in the provinces and hardly any in London.

It was the formation of the National Liberal Federation that really sparked off the grand debate on the merits and defects of the Caucus. For Joseph Chamberlain and his friends the Caucus meant a 'democratisation' of the Liberal Party by, as he wrote, 'the direct participation of all its members in the direction of its policy and in the selection of those particular measures of reform to which priority shall be given' (**97**, p. 133). Such a conception of party organisation implied an attack on the domination of the Whigs within the party, as reflected in both the Leadership and the Whips' Office, and a demand for renewed energy, enthusiasm and purpose within contemporary Liberalism [**doc. 19**]. It was this emphasis on 'action' that appealed to Gladstone, and that led him – obsessed as he was with the Eastern Question – to give the Federation his political blessing by addressing its inaugural meeting in May 1877. Equally typically, Lord Granville warned him against going, and Lord Hartington refused to recognise the Federation at all [**doc. 20**].

If these arch-Whigs damned the Caucus with faint praise, other critics were more forthright in their denunciations. It was argued that the Caucus organisation gave power to a ruthless (and probably corrupt) faction, who not only manipulated the whole Federation in the interests of Birmingham, but through their control of voters, parliamentary candidates and policy would eventually dictate to Parliament itself. Probably the truth is, as Professor Hanham suggests, somewhere between the two extremes (**85**, ch. 7). Certainly, Chamberlain's more extravagant claims on behalf of the 'democracy' of the Caucus were patently absurd, since in practice, if not in theory, power fell more and more into the hands of the Executive Committee, and the Associations soon came to represent no one but themselves. 'The popular form of the party Organisation', in Ostrogorski's harsh judgement, 'merely enables the latter to penetrate deeper into the masses for the purpose of capturing them more easily, and not for giving them independence' (**88**, p. 303).

The machinery of the Caucus did seem to be justified by the Liberal victory in 1880, when Chamberlain and Schnadhorst claimed that the Liberals gained or retained sixty out of sixty-seven constituencies where 'popular' associations existed. The claim was somewhat exaggerated (**93**), but even opponents such as Disraeli and Churchill were impressed. This flush of success, increased by Chamberlain's appointment to the Cabinet in 1880, and the rise in the number of affiliated Associations in the 'eighties, did lead to the Federation asserting itself more forcefully. If it did not yet formulate a party programme and try to impose it on the party leadership, it at least claimed the right to ascertain and express specific policies, such as franchise reform, in accordance with its Conference resolution in 1881. 'A mere telegram from the bigwigs of the Caucus' wrote Ostrogorski with typical exaggeration, 'was enough to set the Associations in motion throughout the country, and the lion growled, screamed, moved with pleasure or with anger as occasion required' (**88**, pp. 209–10).

The beast was soon to be tamed. In 1884 Schnadhorst resigned as Secretary of the Birmingham Liberal Association to become full-time Secretary of the National Liberal Federation; and owing to the influence of Joseph Chamberlain, who was anxious to curb Whig influence at the centre, he was also given a seat on the Standing Committee of the Liberal Central Office – a poacher turned gamekeeper. Two years later, in 1886, he became Secretary of the Central Office also, and the N.L.F.'s headquarters were moved from Birmingham to join it in London. In this way Schnadhorst was able to control the Liberal organisation both nationally and at the centre. But by that time, owing to the split in the party over Home Rule, it was to be used not to increase but to destroy the power of his former master, Joseph Chamberlain (**93**). A new phase in the history of the Liberal Party and the National Liberal Federation began in 1886.

The later nineteenth century

The most important influence on political practice in the later nineteenth century was not party organisation but the great trio of laws passed by the Liberals in the 1880s: the Corrupt and Illegal Practices Act of 1883, the Third Reform Act of 1884 and the Redistribution Act 1885. By effectively limiting election expenses, the first Act transformed 'the whole character of British electioneering within a generation' (**101**, p. 175). It did this in two ways. In the long run it meant that poorer men could become parliamentary candidates; more immediately, it made voluntary work at elections more and more vital, and therefore emphasised the importance of party membership and national, rather than local, standards in the constituencies. The Reform Acts had a similar effect. For the equalising of the franchise in boroughs and counties and the introduction of single-member constituencies throughout the country meant, as Ensor suggests, that 'the individual for the first time became the unit and numerical equality... the master principle' (**2**, p. 88). This was not in fact entirely true in detail (**107**). Nevertheless, the increase in the unity and standardisation of the electoral system, accompanied as it was by the rise of national leaders and national issues in the later years of the nineteenth century, was bound to enlarge also the influence of the party Central Offices. And this fitted in with tendencies operating within the parties themselves.

In the Conservative Party, the end of Lord Randolph Churchill's *mésalliance* with the National Union was followed by its reorganisation, on paper at least. In 1885 every Conservative Association was automatically affiliated to the National Union, and it thus became a really national organisation; in the following year ten Provincial Unions were established. It is true that these reforms were accompanied by the Union Conferences passing resolutions on political subjects, but these were blandly ignored by the party leaders. 'The action of the Conference', in Lowell's famous phrase, 'is not fettered; it is ignored' (**87**). In the later nineteenth century the organisation of the Conservative Party was in fact run harmoniously by three men: Lord Salisbury, the Prime Minister, Akers-Douglas, the Chief Whip, and Captain Middleton. Middleton was both Party Agent and Secretary of the National Union between 1886 and 1903; and, by linking up the two principal sections of the party organisation – tactfully and skilfully – with the Parliamentary Party, the Conservative organisation reached during these years virtually technical perfection. The ascendancy of this remarkable triumvirate meant that the principle of 'authority' within the Conservative Party, never seriously in doubt, had finally triumphed.

So too with the Liberal Party. The fact that the National Liberal Federation remained loyal to Gladstone after 1886, and that thereafter Schnadhorst combined the posts of Secretary of the Federation and the Liberal Central Office until his retirement in 1894, did help to bring the central and local organisations of the Liberal Party closer together. On the other hand the secession of the Whigs in 1886 led

to a rising tide of radicalism in the party which Gladstone was unable to stem, and this was reflected in the growing attempt by the
National Liberal Federation to formulate and commit the party
leaders to a definite programme. The high-water mark of this attitude was the famous 'Newcastle Programme' of 1891: a long and
rambling series of resolutions which the Federation hoped would be
passed into law by the next Liberal Government, 'embodying Reforms which have been declared again and again by this Council to
be essential to the welfare of the people of the United Kingdom'
(**87**, i, 536). Gladstone did, after 1892, legislate on some of
the proposals, though he never explicitly endorsed the programme.
The programme, however, was felt to be an embarrassment to the
Liberal Government, and Rosebery, when he succeeded Gladstone
in 1894, denounced the whole conception of attempting to fetter the
hands of the parliamentary leaders; indeed, he blamed the 'Newcastle Programme' for the downfall of the Government in the following year. Thereafter, in the remaining years of the nineteenth
century, while altering the rules of the National Liberal Federation
to create a pretence of greater power, the Liberal leaders – like
their Conservative counterparts – really secured their own control
over the Liberal Party. 'Both are shams', said Lowell, commenting
on the fate of the Union and the Federation, 'but with this difference, that the Conservative organisation is a transparent, and the
Liberal an opaque, sham' (**87**).

4   The Liberal Crisis

Whigs and Radicals

Turning his back on an ungrateful nation, Gladstone retired as leader of the Liberal Party in 1875, determined to spend his remaining years in theological study and reflection. He was succeeded by a duumvirate: Lord Hartington was elected leader in the Commons, and Lord Granville continued as leader in the House of Lords. But though the radicals had acquiesced in the election of Hartington – Forster was unacceptable owing to his education policy – it was clearly a victory for the conservative and aristocratic section of the Liberal Party. How then could the radicals capture the party? The answer given by Joseph Chamberlain was, as we have seen, to extend and strengthen the system of Liberal Associations that had blossomed after the defeat of 1874, and eventually in 1877 to join them together into the National Liberal Federation.

Curiously, Mr Gladstone attended the famous inaugural meeting of the Federation held at Birmingham on 31 May 1877 – in the very citadel of radical nonconformity. His presence there was a response to Chamberlain's invitation, and Chamberlain's motives in urging him to attend were transparently clear. He intended to reshape the Liberal Party in his own image, and the presence of Gladstone at the Birmingham meeting would help him to do that. As he told Dilke quite frankly: '...at this time I can't help thinking he is our best card...if he were to come back for a few years (he can't continue in public life for very much longer) he would probably do much for us and pave the way for more' (**26**, i, 240). Chamberlain's conviction that Gladstone's retirement was always just around the corner was to betray him time and time again in the course of the next ten years, and to affect profoundly his own fate and that of the Liberal Party. Granville warned Gladstone against going: 'I presume', he wrote, 'that Chamberlain's object is not to reorganise the whole liberal party, but to strengthen the young liberal and more advanced portion of it, and to secure you willing or unwilling as its leader' (**18**, i, 41).

Gladstone was not unaware of Chamberlain's motives; but he argued in reply that any opportunity must be seized for hammering the Conservative Government (**18**, i, 42), and in any case he had his own special reasons for going. For, in the previous year, abandoning his theological studies, he had, under pressure, emerged as the greatest supporter of the Bulgarian Agitation. He soon found, sadly, that his own front bench and official Anglicanism were lukewarm in support, whereas many radicals and the whole of nonconformity were solidly behind him. This impressed Gladstone profoundly; he never forgot what he called their 'noble support', and his visit to Birmingham in 1877 is, in a sense, a public gesture of support and appreciation for English nonconformity which did much to heal the rift that had developed between them over his earlier education policy. It is also something more. It is, as Dr Shannon has argued in his book on the Bulgarian Agitation, in its attempt to rebuild that moral *rapport* with the masses that had been broken in 1874, a stage on the road to Midlothian and the resumption of the Liberal leadership (**23**).

The fundamental conflict between Whigs and radicals, already emerging during the Bulgarian Agitation of 1876, became more defined in the years preceding the general election of 1880. It was symbolised perhaps by Lord Hartington's distaste for the National Liberal Federation, and his refusal to address its annual meeting in 1878, despite Chamberlain's veiled threat: 'Can the leader of the liberal party afford to ignore altogether so large a section of it? If he does, the organisation will necessarily tend more and more to separate from official Liberalism and to form a party within the party' (**22**, i, 246–7). This seemed not unlikely. In the election of 1880 the radicals believed they had two advantages *vis-à-vis* the Whigs. First, the control of the National Liberal Federation; second, the support of Mr Gladstone who was now regarded as almost an 'honorary radical'. The results of the election seemed to offer them the fulfilment of their hopes. The Liberals obtained a majority of 137 over the Conservatives, and the success in many boroughs could be attributed partly to the work of the National Liberal Federation. 'The old Whigs are astonished and bewildered', wrote Frederic Harrison to Charles Dilke. 'They have not won the victory. It has been forced on them by the Radicals, almost against their will.... Gladstone must give support to the Left whether he wishes it or not.'

In this he was over-sanguine. For the fundamental fact about the election of 1880 from the point of view of the Liberal Party was that it was 'Mr Gladstone's victory'; and, as he himself said, 'it made me again leader whether I would or no' (**15**, ii, 158). The enormous prestige he had built up since 1876 enabled him therefore to bypass the radical programme and bend the Liberal Party to his own will. This was something which Lord Hartington would never have had the strength to do if he had continued as leader; and Gladstone's triumph in 1880 was, therefore, in Dr Shannon's phrase, 'the ruin of Radicalism' (**23**). This was indeed implied almost as soon as Gladstone formed his new Government. For only one member of his Cabinet of eleven was a full-blown radical, Chamberlain at the Board of Trade, and Dilke had to make do with the Under-Secretaryship at the Foreign Office. 'From this one-sided start', says Ensor, 'much of Gladstone's failure in his 1880–5 administration may be traced. For never in the modern era has a triumphant House of Commons majority achieved so little (**2**, pp. 66–7).

It was this that disenchanted the radicals with Mr Gladstone within a few years of the great victory of 1880. It is true that there were special reasons for the Prime Minister's tardiness as a reformer. He was faced with problems both in Ireland and overseas which were not only of extraordinary complexity but charged with emotional dynamite; and in the Commons there were the wearying and time-consuming tactics of the Irish and the 'Fourth Party', as well as the wider problem of maintaining the unity of the Liberals. Prior to 1884 none of the great social policies of the radicals – disestablishment, franchise reform, land purchase, tax changes – had been accomplished; Chamberlain had even failed to carry his Merchant Shipping Bill through the Commons. For many radicals, moreover, even more disillusioning than the Government's sins of omission were their sins of commission. It was the Government's coercive policy in Ireland in 1881–82 that many found particularly repugnant: they were even more strongly opposed to what appeared to be a continuation of Disraeli's imperialism in South Africa and, more egregiously, in Egypt and the Sudan. The occupation of Egypt in particular produced a real moral crisis for the Liberal Party: how could armed intervention against a native people be justified on Liberal principles? Indeed on this issue there was no clearcut Whig–Radical division; the radicals themselves were bitterly divided – a portent of what was to come in the 1890s. Chamberlain, though he disliked the reasons for it, supported Hartington in favour of intervention, just as earlier he had in the end supported coercion in Ireland; while radical anti-imperialists like John Morley were strongly against any such action, and John Bright, consistent to the last, resigned from the Government after the bombardment of Alexandria in 1882. Like 1872 in the First, 1882 was in many ways a year of crisis in the history of the Second Liberal Administration. Hartington believed that, over the Egyptian question, the Government was 'in imminent danger of being broken up', and he urged upon Gladstone the duty of carrying on as Premier: 'your retirement would lead to the speedy, if not the immediate, dissolution of the Government and of the present Liberal majority' (**22**, vol. i).

Gladstone had no intention of retiring. The Government was reconstructed, and Dilke was brought into the Cabinet as President of the Local Government Board. This did little to pacify the radicals. 'The Radicals in the Cabinet', Chamberlain wrote of the year 1883, 'were now only Dilke and myself and we found our views ignored or outvoted by the majority of our colleagues. In the country, however, our opinions were endorsed by at least four-fifths of the Liberal Party' (**29**, p. 86). It was this that led many radicals in the country to demand a more vigorous campaign by Chamberlain against the domination of the Whigs. But Chamberlain believed that there were sound reasons for his refusal to force things to an issue with the Hartingtons and Granvilles. The radicals were still a minority in the Cabinet and in the Parliamentary Party; and – like the Whigs also – they still needed, as Edward Hamilton observed, 'Mr G's aegis to be spread over them'. Chamberlain's plan, therefore, was to postpone the battle for control of the party until a general election could be fought, after the passing of a new Reform Act; then, with the country labourers enfranchised and the constituencies remodelled, the radicals could dominate the party and he would emerge as Party Leader, for Gladstone was then bound to retire. Chamberlain's plan worked, almost. For when the Reform Acts *were* passed in 1884–85, the establishment of single-member constituencies – which ended the old practice by which a Whig and a radical were run together in two-member constituencies – did mark, *vis-à-vis* the Whigs, a radical triumph, though it probably helped the Conservatives even more. What the editor of the radical *Fortnightly* called the 'Revolution of 1884' meant, as he affirmed, that 'the buffers on which timid Liberalism has hitherto relied against advanced Liberalism will henceforth disappear' (**32**).

The Whigs, however, were not necessarily prepared to await their fate passively. If the radicals were soon disenchanted with Mr Gladstone so too, for very different reasons, were many Whigs.

Suspicious already, even before the formation of his second ministry, of Gladstone's dallying with 'democracy', his Irish policy seemed to confirm their worst fears. The Land Act of 1870, said Ramsden, was to be treated as 'the thin end of the wedge ... [to] shatter the whole fabric of land–tenant relations by successive blows' (**21**, p. 373). Even worse was the Second Land Act which Hartington found 'a hard morsel to swallow' (**22**, i, 340). Not only did it attack the landlords' just rights in Ireland, but its likely effects in England were even more alarming. For there the landlords were already under fire politically from every species of land reformer – in the spirit of Chamberlain's famous denunciation of them in 1883 as 'the class that toil not neither do they spin' – at the very moment when, economically, they were hit by fierce agricultural depression (**117**). Nor indeed was it only the landed interest that found itself menaced by the spirit of Gladstone's legislation. A representative of the important 'city interest' in the Liberal Party like Goschen (who had ostentatiously refused to join the Government in 1880) was equally uneasy, as indeed were many small property owners, an important factor in the Conservative reaction of the later nineteenth century.

As a result of these developments the Whig revulsion against Gladstonian Liberalism began even before the great secession of 1886. Sixty Whig peers revolted against the Government over the Irish Compensation Bill in 1880, entitling us, says Dr Southgate, 'to regard the vote as a rehearsal by the Whig peerage of its exit from the Liberal ranks, which so many now saw as a matter of time only' (**21**, p. 372). The Irish Land Bill of 1881 was originally defeated in the Lords by 282 to 51, and would have been defeated even if no Tory had voted. Lord Lansdowne resigned from the Government in 1880; the Duke of Argyle a year later over the Land Bill, and Lord Cowper (and W. E. Forster) in 1882: the 'Revolt of the Whigs' had begun (**81**).

The year 1885 saw, therefore, what was really an intense struggle between the Whigs and radicals for control of the Liberal Party. This was accompanied in the early part of the year by tentative moves within the Cabinet aimed at ousting the Prime Minister and establishing a Hartington administration supported by Chamberlain and Dilke (**40**). This was a response to the apparent collapse of Gladstone's political morale (and his health) as a result of the agonising problems of Egyptian finance, and General Gordon and the Sudan. By the spring, however, the Prime Minister had recovered his nerve, following the fall of Khartoum in February, and reasserted his authority upon the Cabinet. In May, however, Chamberlain and Dilke tendered their resignations over the question of renewing the Irish Crimes Bill; but this action was overtaken by events when, a few weeks later, the Government was defeated by a combination of Irish and Conservative votes, with more than seventy Liberals abstaining. Gladstone resigned, and was succeeded by a Conservative 'Caretaker Government' under Lord Salisbury until, when the new electoral lists had been compiled, a general election could be held. The election campaign at the end of the year was virtually a personal duel between Lord Hartington and Joseph Chamberlain, a duel in which the radical set the pace. For Chamberlain, aware of the disappointment of his supporters with the achievements of the Government of which he had been a prominent member, now hoped to renew their morale with a campaign for a definite 'Radical Programme' (**30**), a programme which was developed in detail in a great cycle of speeches throughout the country in 1885, much to the discomfiture of Gladstone who was uneasy about Chamberlain's methods and loath to see the party committed to such definite policies [**doc. 21**]. Chamberlain's original Radical Programme, however, was considerably modified in the course of the year until, during the election, under the sobriquet of the 'Unauthorised Programme', it consisted for Chamberlain of four major points: local government reform, land reform, free education and tax reform (**28**). On paper, this did not differ all that much from Gladstone's 'Authorised' programme published in September, which also included proposals on local government and tax reform, but it was interpreted as a sop to the Whigs. 'It is a slap in the face to us', wrote Chamberlain to Dilke. 'His reign cannot be a long one.... If we chose to go into direct opposition we might smash him but the game is not worth the candle' (**26**, ii, 96).

The Whigs, however, were still alarmed, professing to see in Chamberlain's proposals the spectre of 'Socialism', though Chamberlain – who believed profoundly that his proposed reforms would stimulate individual, and especially local, effort – was not really a Socialist at all (**27**, p. 46). In reply to Chamberlain's attacks Lord Hartington defended the 'rights of property' in a notable speech at Waterfoot in August; and in October he wrote despondently, but prophetically, to Granville: 'Of course in the long run the active men will have their own way and the future Liberal Party will be Radical. I see nothing for the Whigs but to disappear or turn Tories' (**22**, ii, 74). That sea-change was not to take place, yet. For though Gladstone was in many ways antipathetic to Chamberlain –

'his socialism repels me,' he said – he was perhaps even more dis-illusioned with the conduct of 'the timid or reactionary Whigs' (**15**, ii, 461–2). He tried desperately, therefore, with his mind already turning towards Ireland, to maintain at least some semblance of unity in the party; and the final showdown between Chamberlain and the Whigs failed to take place before the Liberals faced the general election of November 1885. 'The problem for me', wrote Gladstone, 'is to make if possible a statement which will hold through the election, and not to go into conflict with either the right wing of the party, for whom Hartington has spoken, or the left wing... for whom Chamberlain spoke' (**45**).

That election – one of the oddest in modern British political his-tory – did little to rejoice the hearts of either Whigs, Radicals or Conservatives. The final figures were: Liberal 335, Conservatives 249, Irish 86; and the real victor was Parnell, who had not only obtained his primary aim – to hold the balance of power in the House of Commons – but had utterly destroyed the power of the Liberal Party in Ireland into the bargain. One of the outstanding features of the election from the Liberals' point of view was their heavy losses in the boroughs. It is true that they still maintained their lead in the largest industrial cities, but in London, Lancashire and the smaller boroughs generally they did badly. This was due to a variety of causes. Lord Grosvenor, the Chief Whip, believed that Chamberlain's 'extremism' had 'frightened away shoals' of floating voters; certainly recent historians find his electoral campaign in 1885 curiously inept (**39, 40, 112**).

Gladstone himself wrote to Grosvenor that the main factors were: 'Fair Trade + Parnell + Church + Chamberlain... I place the *causae damni* in what I think their order of importance' (**25**, p. 398). This was a fair estimate. The Catholic workingmen in Eng-land obediently voted Conservative in accordance with Parnell's instructions, and this was particularly important in Lancashire. But there is also some evidence to suggest that the industrial work-ing classes in the cities were strongly influenced by the unsatisfac-tory state of trade; and it is worth emphasising that many of them saw Joseph Chamberlain not so much as the supporter of the 'Un-authorised Programme' (in which they had little interest) but as the ex-President of the Board of Trade who had done little to im-prove their prospects of employment. Nor was it only the fact that he had no 'urban cow' (in Labouchère's famous phrase) to offer them that accounts for the coolness of the workers towards Cham-berlain: most of their leaders had resented him from the start. 'The

Radical today', said J. E. Williams of the Social Democratic Federation, 'was the "Artful Dodger" who went up and down the country telling the people to take hold of the landlord thief but to let the greater thief, the capitalist, go scotfree' (**125**, p. 53).

In the counties, on the other hand, the Liberals did remarkably well: in England and Wales their numbers went up from 54 in 1880 to 133 in 1885 – giving them about thirty more county seats than their Conservative opponents. This is generally attributed to Chamberlain's wooing of the agricultural labourer – enfranchised in 1884 – with his land policy, the famous 'three acres and a cow'; but Mr Pelling is more sceptical. He believes that the growing Conservative support of protection was more important, and the agricultural labourer voted Liberal 'more out of fear of fiscal change, which might increase the cost of living, than because of any positive attraction of Chamberlain's social programme' (**100**, p. 16). Clearly, bread and butter issues were again of major importance in an election. It was Irish policy, however, that determined what party should now govern. Immediately after the election in November Lord Salisbury, with the tacit support of the Irish Party, carried on as Prime Minister. But in December Herbert Gladstone flew his 'Hawarden Kite' and announced to a startled world the news of his father's conversion to Home Rule. Soon after Parliament reassembled in January 1886, therefore, the Irish switched their votes and Gladstone, at the age of seventy-seven, became Prime Minister for the third time, committed in fact, if not yet formally, to a policy of Home Rule for Ireland.

Ireland

It had taken Gladstone many years of anguish and reflection before he reached the conclusion that Home Rule was the only solution for the Irish problem. Though he took up the Irish question in 1868 as a response to the Fenian outrages and as a device for uniting his party, he did so also, as he told his sister, 'in the name of the God of truth and justice' (**24**). It is his concern with 'justice for Ireland' that is the *leitmotiv* of J. L. Hammond's classic study of 'Gladstone and the Irish Nation'. (**25**). But it is not unfair to suggest that for the Liberal leader 'Ireland was viewed in a context of deep party calculation' (**40**).

The aim of Gladstone's early Irish reforms was simply 'to pacify Ireland': to wipe out specific grievances over land and religion by legislative action and thus justify to the Irish people the wisdom of the Union. There was as yet no firm conviction that beneath the complexities of church endowments and land tenures there were deeper more fundamental problems for Ireland and England. This attitude still governed Gladstone's approach to the question in the later 'seventies despite the rise of crime and violence in Ireland, the outcome of a new cycle of evictions in response to agricultural depression. Nor was his resolution altered by the so-called 'new departure' of 1879 – the formation of the Land League, and the beginning of Parnell's mastery of the Irish Parliamentary Party. In that year it was the crimes of 'Beaconsfieldism' elsewhere than on the other side of St George's Channel that obsessed his mind (**52**).

Hence when Gladstone assumed the premiership for the second time in 1880, he was still thinking in terms of clearing up one or two difficult problems, mainly in foreign and imperial affairs, before returning to that 'quiet and unobtrusive life' (as he expressed it to Rosebery in 1878) from which he had been so rudely snatched in 1876. As he admitted frankly in 1884 with reference to Ireland: 'I did not know, no one knew, the severity of the crisis that was already swelling upon the horizon, and that shortly after rushed upon us like a flood' (**15**, ii, 288). What changed his attitude after 1880 was his growing awareness that in Ireland the government faced not just a 'political' but a 'social' revolution as a result of the activities of the Land League (**15**, ii, 287). The only long-term solution to this was, as he insisted in opposition to Forster, not the imprisonment of a handful of so-called agitators, but large-scale land and local government reform. 'Until we have', he told the Irish Secretary in 1882, 'seriously responsible bodies to deal with us in Ireland, every plan we frame comes to Irishmen...as an English plan. As such it is probably condemned.... It is liberty alone which fits men for liberty' (**15**, ii, 298). It is from sentiments such as these that we can already discern the shadowy outlines of Gladstone's later Home Rule policy.

Unhappily for Gladstone, his position after 1880 was very unsatisfactory for initiating a new phase of reform for Ireland; even apart from other considerations further Irish reform was bound to antagonise in some way both wings of the Liberal Party. The Whigs, as we have seen, were fearful of any further attacks on the landlords' powers; while for the radicals, even when they strongly supported the Prime Minister's specific proposals, such a programme was bound to be regarded as a gigantic red herring – an alternative to the vital social reforms needed so badly at home. Gladstone's Irish policy, therefore, during his second ministry, though well-meaning, failed on two counts. It failed on the one hand, despite the merits of individual measures like the Second Land Act or the proposed extension of local government, to satisfy the national aspirations of the Irish people; while, on the other hand, every major Irish proposal introduced served only to exacerbate animosities and disagreements within the Liberal Cabinet. By the time the ministry came to an end in June 1885, therefore, Gladstone was convinced that traditional Liberal policy towards Ireland was completely bankrupt.

It was this that helped to make the summer months of 1885 the key period in Gladstone's conversion to Home Rule. His own policy of religious and agrarian reform had failed to reconcile the Irish to the continuance of English rule; further reform was bound to be just as nugatory. Moreover, Gladstone's reflection during these months on the fundamentals of the Irish attitude, coupled with his deep 'European' outlook, convinced him of the reality of Irish nationality: how then could he oppose what a majority of the Irish people wanted [**doc. 22**]? His letters to Hartington and Chamberlain in September showed that it was perfectly plain to them that his mind was moving to a definite Home Rule policy (**25**, pp. 404–6). The problem for Gladstone was – what tactics should he now pursue? In the end he determined, publicly, to maintain silence over his conversion to Home Rule. Why? Gladstone seems to have been moved primarily by two considerations. In the first place, if he spoke out publicly in favour of Home Rule the break-up of the Liberal Party would inevitably follow, and on the eve of a general election; in addition, he could be accused of counterbidding for the Irish vote. Secondly, as J. L. Hammond has argued, Gladstone aimed, sincerely if naïvely, at achieving a non-party approach to the Irish problem. The Conservatives had after all come into power in June 1885 as a result of Parnell's conviction that he could get more from them than from the Liberals. As a result, coercion *was* dropped, a land purchase policy *was* successfully inaugurated; might not this lead on therefore – following feelers put out by Carnarvon, the Irish Viceroy – to a Conservative policy of Home Rule? Gladstone realised, moreover, the enormous advantages for the success of a Home Rule policy if it was introduced by Lord Salisbury, with his mastery of the House of Lords, backed up by the majority of Liberals. 'Every step he took between June 1885 and January 1886', writes J. L. Hammond, 'was a deliberate effort to obtain a solution by passionless cooperation among the leading statesmen' (**25**, p. 471). It was these considerations that led Gladstone to keep silence, even to Parnell and his colleagues, during the election campaign at the end of the year, and to acquiesce in Irish support for the Conservative Party.

The outcome of the election of 1885 was a disappointment for Gladstone in so far as it failed to provide either of the English parties with a real majority independent of the Irish members. On the other hand, the fact that the Irish Party won every seat in Ireland south of Ulster clinched his support for Home Rule. 'I consider that Ireland has now spoken', he wrote to Hartington on 17 December, 'and that an effort ought to be made *by the government* without delay to meet her demands for the management by an Irish legislative body of Irish as distinct from imperial affairs. Only a government can do it, and a tory government can do it more easily and safely than any other' (**15**, ii, 503). Gladstone's hope, however, was utterly destroyed by the publication on the very same day of the news of his support for Home Rule, as a result of the deliberate action of his son, Herbert Gladstone. Herbert believed that Chamberlain and his radical friends were planning to take over the Liberal Party, and the only way to forestall them was by flying the 'Hawarden Kite' and forcing his father to re-enter the political arena. As a result, it was Gladstone and not Salisbury who faced the formidable task of forming a government at the end of January to introduce Home Rule for Ireland. Nor was Gladstone himself unaware perhaps of the personal and party implications of these events. 'The (Home Rule) bill', write Cooke and Vincent, 'was meant to unite the Liberal party by committing it to the principle of home rule and to prepare it for further protracted struggle in which there would be only one possible leader' (**40**).

It was a task undertaken in the worst possible circumstances since nearly all his colleagues had been left completely in the dark about this change of attitude. Hartington and most of the ex-Whig ministers refused to join; Chamberlain and Trevelyan did so reluctantly, but resigned in March once the Home Rule Bill was introduced before the Cabinet. 'What happened in 1886', writes J. L. Hammond, 'was exactly the opposite of what Gladstone wanted in 1885. . . . For the crisis created a combination, but a combination not to obtain reform but to defeat it' (**25**, pp. 456–7). This it did in June 1886 when ninety-three Liberal Unionists, led by Lord Hartington and Joseph Chamberlain, combined with the Conservatives in the House of Commons to defeat the Home Rule Bill. How are we to explain their opposition?

About the Whigs, and indeed many moderate Liberals, there is no great problem. For them, as Dr Southgate suggests, Home Rule was the occasion rather than the cause of the split in the Liberal Party, for it seemed to be the apotheosis of all those features of contemporary 'democracy' about which they were most uneasy. 'What Home Rule did', he writes, 'was to turn the growing trickle of seceders into a flood, by presenting a major and dramatic issue' (**21**, p. 414). This is clearly true for Lord Hartington. In the 1880s he became increasingly restless at Gladstonian policy, and felt that he was fighting a losing battle with the radicals – only loyalty and awe of Gladstone kept him in the Cabinet. The real problem is Joseph Chamberlain, and his behaviour in the Home Rule crisis is the most puzzling and controversial of all. For Joseph Chamberlain was after all a radical, in Irish as well as in domestic affairs. It was Chamberlain who in 1881 originally supported Gladstone in opposing Forster's proposed Coercion Bill, and in the following year acted as a link between the Cabinet and Parnell in arranging the 'Kilmainham Treaty'. It was Chamberlain further who, in 1885, was the principal opponent within the Cabinet of an unconditional renewal of the Irish Crimes Act, and who attempted, through O'Shea, to obtain Parnell's agreement to a Central Board Scheme which would give the Irish wide-ranging powers of internal control (**21**, pp. 366–7). It was indeed over Irish affairs that he and Dilke tendered their resignations in May of that year.

Why then was it Chamberlain of all people who allied with his old Whig enemy, Hartington, in 1886, to oppose Gladstone's Home Rule Bill? A number of points may be suggested. In the first place, it is impossible to ignore the factor of personality. Though each recognised the high qualities of the other, there was that lack of real sympathy and understanding between Gladstone and Chamberlain which was bound to make agreement more difficult in dealing with the intractable problems of Ireland; and the fault here lies mainly with Gladstone. The 'Grand Old Man' was tactless and insensitive in his relations with his younger colleague. He was loath to admit him to the Cabinet in 1880; in 1882 he twice failed to consider him for the post of Irish Secretary when in many ways Chamberlain would have been an admirable choice; even in 1885, when Chamberlain was anxious to become Colonial Secretary, he was first absurdly offered the Admiralty, and then given the Local Government Board but without any strong backing for a policy of social reform. All this meant not only that Chamberlain felt, with considerable justification, that he was being slighted at the behest of the Whigs, but also that he was not bound by the same ties of personal devotion and loyalty to Gladstone which characterised the behaviour of many Liberals in 1886, including even a Whig like Granville.

But quite apart from personal differences, the two men looked at Ireland in fundamentally different ways. Gladstone did eventually attempt, if with only partial success, to see Irish problems through Irish eyes; Chamberlain made no real attempt to view Ireland other than as an Englishman, and a nonconformist at that. What Chamberlain increasingly emphasised after 1881 was not the causes but the harsh reality of Irish crime and violence, and the callousness and duplicity of the Irish leaders [**doc. 23**]. Implicit in Chamberlain's approach, therefore, was the view that the Irish were unfit to govern themselves – at least in important matters; and this view appeared to be confirmed by Parnell's double-dealing over the Central Board Scheme (though the fault here lay with O'Shea), and his untrustworthiness in switching the Irish vote in the 1885 election. It is this almost instinctive belief in strong efficient government at almost any price – as typical of his early radical as of his later Conservative career – that helps to explain Chamberlain's attitude towards Home Rule. He was prepared to go far, as his Central Board Scheme shows, in giving the Irish what he believed they wanted: as he said, 'the widest possible self-government...consistent with the integrity of the Empire' (**29**, p. 151); but, unlike Gladstone, he was not prepared to make the jump (and the gap seemed a very small one to many contemporaries) from devolution to Home Rule, even if a majority of Irishmen clearly wanted it. The disruption of the Empire which would, he argued, inevitably follow, was too high a price to pay. In any case he believed that such purely political considerations were really irrelevant. It was the land question that was 'the foundation of Irish...discontent and should be settled first' (**29**, p. 229).

There is one last point. How sincere, even in these terms, was Chamberlain's opposition to Home Rule? Chamberlain in his own *Political Memoir*, written mainly in 1892, sees himself as a man who put country and Empire before party loyalty and personal ambition in the crisis of 1886; and this is a view which his principal biographer, J. L. Garvin, follows. But it is difficult to believe that Joseph Chamberlain was not also conscious of the long-term political advantages of what he was doing – as more recent historians have implied; and once again his belief in the imminent retirement of Gladstone was crucial. For Chamberlain was well aware of the antipathy of the British public – and particularly the working-men –

to the Irish, and therefore to Home Rule, a theme he constantly stressed in private correspondence throughout the 'eighties. If the Liberal Party came out in support of Home Rule at a new general election, he suggested to Gladstone in 1885, 'it is my belief that we should sustain a tremendous defeat. The English working classes, for various reasons, are distinctly hostile to Home Rule carried to this extent' (**29**, p. 171). Hence there was much to be said for the view that, if the Liberal train was bent on destruction, then it would be wise for Chamberlain, temporarily, to get off and come back later to take over the controls from Gladstone after his inevitable retirement. This interpretation certainly seems to be implicit in the important letter he wrote to his brother on 8 March 1886 [**doc. 24**]. This view would imply further that he was determined to kill the Home Rule Bill come what may, and that Chamberlain's negotiations with Gladstone over its detailed provisions were a mere smokescreen. Indeed, he wrote to Dilke on 6 May 1886: 'To satisfy others I have talked about conciliation, and have consented to make advances, but on the whole I would rather vote against the Bill than not, and the retention of the Irish members is only with me, the flag that covers other objections' (**25**, p. 495). In the end, of course, things did not work out quite as Chamberlain expected. The Home Rule Bill *was* defeated; the Unionists *did* win a great victory at the polls in the general election of July 1886; but the G.O.M. stubbornly refused to bow to the inevitable. What destroyed Chamberlain's plans, therefore, was Gladstone's determination to carry on as Liberal leader after 1886, and the willpower and obstinacy that enabled him to do so for another eight years. By that time any hope of Chamberlain rejoining the Liberal Party had long since passed.

After 1886

The decline of the Liberal Party is the major feature of Victorian political history between 1886 and the death of the Queen. The facts seem to speak for themselves, though they are difficult to interpret. In the general election that followed the defeat of the Home Rule Bill in 1886 the Unionists won a resounding victory, winning 394 seats (316 Conservatives, 78 Liberal Unionists); the Gladstonian Liberals were reduced to 191, backed up by the Irish Party of 85 members. This verdict may reasonably be regarded as exceptional since it followed immediately upon the split in the Liberal Party. But even at the general election of 1892, though the Liberals increased their numbers, their parliamentary majority was obtained only by complete dependence on the Irish members: Liberals 273, Irish 81, Conservatives 269, Liberal Unionists 46. In the election of 1895, by which time the repercussions of Home Rule were practically dead, the Liberals suffered their worst defeat of the century. They lost about 100 seats, while the Conservatives and their Liberal Unionist allies obtained 411 seats, with an overall majority of 152. The 'Khaki Election' of 1900 barely altered the relative position of the parties. Two general features of the Liberal electoral position during this period are worth emphasising. First, their only parliamentary majority during this period, in 1892, was secured only with the direct support of the Irish Party and the indirect support of Welsh and Scottish voters; they failed to secure a majority of seats in English constituencies. Thereafter, their dependence on the 'Celtic fringe' became even greater, and they were unable to win a majority of English seats until 1906. Second, the weak parliamentary position of the Liberal Party after 1885 was not the consequence of a great slump in the Liberal vote; indeed, even in 1895 they polled nearly two million votes – a little less than in 1892 – and the Conservatives gained only 51 per cent of the total votes cast (**90**, p. 255). The real trouble for the Liberals was that, unlike the Conservatives, they failed to enlarge their absolute poll at a time when the working-class electorate was rapidly increasing; and indeed the fact that the Liberal vote in 1906 was bumped up by about a million, suggests that many working-class 'Liberals' in the later nineteenth century just failed to turn out at elections (**106**) [**doc. 25**].

How are we to explain these facts? One obvious explanation for the decline of the Liberal Party lies in the Home Rule crisis of 1886 and the secession of the Liberal Unionists which followed. Certainly the leadership of the party was dramatically affected, since at one blow both Hartington and Chamberlain were removed, and the prospective succession to Gladstone was drastically altered and, as soon became apparent, weakened. The G.O.M. himself carried on as the leader of the party, still determined to place Irish Home Rule first even if it meant dragging a reluctant rank-and-file along behind him and accepting as a *quid pro quo* the ragbag policies of the 'Newcastle Programme' (**39**). 'The defects of his strength grow on him', wrote Rosebery, 'All black is very black, all white very white' (**35**). But for the English people Gladstone was still, despite his growing remoteness from political realities, the personification of English Liberalism; and after the election of 1892 he became Prime Minister for the fourth time, determined to introduce yet another Home Rule Bill. The Second Bill passed through the Commons in 1893, but was crushed overwhelmingly in the Lords. Gladstone would have liked to dissolve and appeal to the country, as in 1886, but his colleagues – divided by their own personal animosities and strained almost beyond endurance by the G.O.M.'s contemptuous treatment of them – refused to agree; and Gladstone carried on as Premier for another seven wretched months, growing ever more oracular, aloof, embittered, and impossible to work with. The end came in March 1894 when Gladstone, at odds with the whole Cabinet over the naval estimates, at last reluctantly retired [**doc. 26**].

The Liberal Cabinet now faced the extraordinarily difficult problem of finding a successor. In effect the choice was between the Chancellor of the Exchequer, Sir William Harcourt, a man of considerable parliamentary experience and ability, but of an abrasive personality, and the Foreign Secretary, Lord Rosebery, with John Morley, the Irish Secretary, as third runner and go-between. In the end Rosebery emerged as victor, mainly because, despite the obvious weaknesses of his character and position, Harcourt was personally unendurable as Premier to all the Liberal front bench, and Rosebery was the Queen's first choice. Thus, with his ex-rival and bitter enemy leading the party in the House of Commons, he entered upon his *damnosa hereditas*. 'The Liberal schism', Rosebery's latest biographer writes, 'opened the way to his succession as leader of the party by eliminating virtually all his rivals, but ensured that that leadership would be a precarious and compromised position' (**35**, p. 191). That position, difficult from the start, soon became virtually intolerable, as Rosebery described to the Queen in a bitter and revealing letter [**doc. 27**] It was his growing feeling of personal frustration and impotence, rather than the more fundamental weaknesses in the government and party, that led Rosebery to resign on a trivial issue in June 1895. The smash-up of the Liberal Party in the election that followed seemed a just verdict on a Government that had revealed so nakedly its lack of unity, leadership or clearcut policies. 'The firm of Rosebery and Harcourt', as the former wrote to Gladstone with characteristic candour, 'was a fraud upon the public.'

But no real attempt was made by the two men to overcome their differences in the course of the next year. The feud was in fact worsened by growing disputes over foreign and imperial policy in which Gladstone, launching a mini-crusade over Armenia, supported the anti-Rosebery faction: abruptly in October 1896 Rosebery resigned as leader of the Liberal Party. Harcourt, therefore, at last became *de facto* leader; but it soon became only too clear that he was incapable of remedying the deep-seated malaise that afflicted the Liberal Party [**doc. 28**]. His inept performance over the Jameson Raid inquiry convinced his colleagues that he possessed none of the qualities of real leadership, and there were murmurings against him in the National Liberal Federation (**34**). In December 1898, therefore, Harcourt also resigned, to be followed a month later by John Morley's retirement from the Liberal front bench. The removal from active politics of the irresolute trio of Rosebery, Harcourt and Morley, paved the way for the emergence of the dark horse, Henry Campbell-Bannerman, who in the end turned out to be a better political leader than all three. His election to the leadership in February 1899 begins a new period in the history of the Liberal Party.

These quarrels among the Liberal leaders were to some extent at least a reflection of deeper doubts and divisions within the party itself over policy, aims and tactics. What was the *raison d'être* of the Liberal party in a post-Gladstonian world? That was the question that haunted the minds of Liberal politicians and publicists during these years.

In a notable study Professor Hamer has argued that the Victorian Liberal Party was essentially a coalition of disparate elements – nonconformists, trade unionists, temperance reformers, secularists, Home Rulers – united by no common ideology, each section demanding that priority and party support be given to its particular demands (**46**). The Liberal leadership was therefore engaged in a continuous search for some formula that would introduce coherence and unity into a party which always threatened to degenerate into absolute chaos. Professor Hamer interprets the history of Victorian Liberalism in terms of a perpetual tension between two suggested solutions to this problem. On the one hand, the notion of 'the one great cause' – of which Irish Home Rule after 1886 is the outstanding example – which all sections of the party could accept as superior to their immediate and separate aims and unite around. On the other hand, 'programme politics', by which the Liberal Party would commit itself to a definite legislative programme embracing the formulae of all the Liberal sections but giving priority to none. The 'Newcastle Programme' of 1891 is the classical example of this type of commitment, though Irish Home Rule did inevitably head the list.

In the development of this latter strategy Professor Hamer sees 1894 as a key date. He writes:

The sudden removal of the two factors which had disciplined and concentrated Liberal politics over the eight years since 1886 – Gladstone's leadership and the preoccupation with clearing the Irish 'obstruction' – restored to view the basic disorganisation of Liberal politics. Sectionalism re-emerged, rampant and uncontrollable (**46**).

It is this reversion to 'faddism', with each Liberal section pursuing its own hare oblivious of the rest of the field, that Hamer sees as one of the major sources of Liberal weakness in later Victorian England. Land reform; Welsh disestablishment; temperance reform; London 'progressivism'; the 'rights of labour' – these were some of the fads taken up by Liberal factions during these years. 'Liberal Imperialism', the most intellectually distinguished of them all, began as an attempt to provide a new cohesive philosophy for the Liberal Party based on a commitment to 'national' rather than 'sectional' issues. Led by Lord Rosebery and supported by the brilliant trio of Asquith, Grey and Haldane, the Liberal Imperialists argued in favour of a combination of 'sane imperialism', 'national efficiency' and 'social welfare', all resting on the foundation of a stronger and more responsive State (**53**). These ideas implied the notion of 'the clean slate', as Rosebery expressed it in his notorious speech at Chesterfield in December 1901; meaning, the downgrading in Liberal policy of unpopular and out-of-date shibboleths, notably Home Rule (**51**). But the 'Liberal Imperialists' were and remained an *élite*, out of touch with grass-roots feeling – as their over-zealous support for the Boer War showed – and in no position therefore to convert the party to their creed. 'Liberal Imperialism' too ended up as a section, a position which was formalised by the foundation of the Liberal League in 1902.

One should not exaggerate the debilitating consequences of sectionalism during this period. Some historians have argued (in opposition to Hamer) that sectionalism could be a source of strength as well as weakness for the Liberal party. It helped to associate Liberalism with new invigorating ideas and forces within late Victorian England, more particularly in relation to social questions and Celtic nationalism, and provided fresh channels for the flow of Liberal zeal and vitality. These years were the seed-bed of the 'New Liberalism' (**39, 49**).

If the problems of Liberal Party leadership and policy were worsened by the secession of 1886, so too was the more mundane problem of party organisation. This was a problem that was acute enough in any case owing to the electoral reforms of 1884 and 1885 – which increased the size of the electorate and the number of constituencies – and the democratisation of local government which followed the Acts of 1888 and 1894. But it was worsened by the exodus of men of wealth and influence from the ranks of the Liberal Party as a result of the Home Rule crisis. This meant that the whole work of local Liberal Associations in opposing the 'pull' of Conservative influence, particularly in the rural areas, was jeopardised; and, in an age when members of parliament were unpaid and parliamentary candidates were still expected to contribute to election expenses, the Liberal Associations and the Central Office were faced with greater financial burdens and greater difficulties in finding suitable men. The result was, writes Halévy, that 'the party was obliged to be content with second rate candidates, cranks and men inspired by personal ambitions, political adventurers greedy of spoils and honours' (**3**, p. 7). Halévy provides no details, but it is true that the sale of honours was, to some extent, deliberately increased by the Liberal Government of 1892–95 (**121**). What is quite clear, however, is that the Liberal Party now found it beyond its strength to contest every reasonable constituency in the country. Whereas up to 1886 there was no marked difference between the two parties in the number of unopposed seats, after that date the number of seats unopposed by the Liberals increased considerably. In 1895, for example, the Liberals allowed 114 Conservatives to be returned unopposed (compared with only 10 Liberals); in 1900 the figure was 138 (compared with 22 Liberals) (**104**). It was only in 1906 that, as in so many other ways, the advantages of the two parties were reversed.

It is probable that the effects of the schism of 1886 on the fortunes of the Liberal Party have been exaggerated, especially as the National Liberal Federation remained loyal to Gladstone. For there is some evidence to suggest that there were long-term trends at work in the later nineteenth century which were in any case undermining the electoral strength of the party; though these, it must be admitted, are difficult to assess in detail since the constituency history of Great Britain during this period is, with a few notable exceptions, largely *terra incognita*.

One trend, however, which both historians and contemporary observers have commented on is the drift of the middle classes away from the Liberal towards the Conservative Party. This was a tendency which, as we saw earlier, could already be discerned in the election of 1868 and, even more impressively, in 1874, as a result of the whittling away of middle-class grievances by the great reforms of the mid-Victorian period, and the increasing identification of middle-class interests with those of the propertied classes generally, particularly in their suspicion of working-class demands [**doc. 6**]. This meant that by 1880 the Liberals had largely lost suburbia; by 1885 the Conservatives had established a position of equality with the Liberals in the English boroughs; and thereafter the Liberal position worsened *vis-à-vis* the middle class as a result of the considerable advantage the Conservative Party gained by the establishment of single-member constituencies in 1885, and the events of 1886. As Professor Cornford puts it succinctly: 'With the extension of the suffrage class was becoming the most important single factor in deciding political allegiance' (**63**).

The problem for the Liberal Party in the 1890s, therefore, was to try and hold on to its middle-class supporters while increasing its support among the new working-class voters. This was particularly urgent for the party since the traditional nonconformist liberal bloc was a wasting asset, whereas working-class organisation and militancy – over one million members were enrolled in trade unions by 1893 – were rapidly increasing, and could be used perhaps to revitalise the Liberal Party. Unfortunately, during this decade the Liberal Party conspicuously failed to win over the urban working class, as Mr Paul Thompson has shown in detail in the key area of Greater London. 'The loss of London', as he suggests, 'was as serious to the Liberals as that of Birmingham, and a major cause of the long Conservative ascendancy after 1886' (**131**, p. 90). Nor did the Liberals fare much better in a mixed urban–rural area as evidence from Northamptonshire seems to indicate (**98**).

Why then did the Liberal Party fail to increase its hold over the working class in the 'nineties? Part of its failure was a failure of organisation; and money, as we have already seen, was at the heart of it. 'One of the chief causes of this want of proper organisation', wrote the Liberal Central Office, 'is the poverty of many of the constituencies ... [where] the Liberal Party is composed of working men' (**131**, p. 94). But the main answer lies in the failure of the Liberal Party to adapt itself to the needs of a new age. For by 1885–86 the major task of Gladstonian Liberalism, so far as the working class was concerned – the achievement of democratic rights – had been accomplished; the workers, both in town and country, now wanted more attention paid to their immediate bread-and-butter needs in an age of rapid economic change, bitter industrial strife and widening social horizons (**115**). The failure to recognise these aspirations, and to do for the Liberal Party what Disraeli had tried earlier to do for the Conservative Party, was partly a failure of Liberal leadership. Harcourt, despite his radical budgets, had little understanding of or sympathy with trade unionism (**37**); Morley was dogmatically and defiantly a Gladstonian in social and economic affairs (**31**); even Rosebery, who had built up something of a reputation as a social reformer while Chairman of the London County Council, and who saw clearly enough the overwhelming need for the party to break away from the spell of Gladstone, lacked either the power or the will to do much about it. He was enough of an aristocrat in any case to be apprehensive about Harcourt's budget proposals, and to deprecate any attempt to turn the Liberals into a 'popular' party which 'would rest on nothing but a working-class support, without the variety and richness and intellectual forces which used to make up that party' (**35**, p. 342). His government even failed to take seriously the party's proposal for the payment of members of Parliament. Rosebery's own interests as a minister lay, of course, primarily in foreign and imperial policy, but his own brand of Liberal Imperialism made a negligible appeal to working men, and could not in any case compete effectively with the dynamic creed of Joseph Chamberlain. Moreover, the personal feuds and hatreds of the men at the top largely vitiated any real attempt to reshape Liberal policy between 1894 and 1898. As the historian of their squabbles has written: their policies 'lacked coherence, consistency and a clearly defined aim. They wasted themselves in trivialities' (**37**, p. 173).

The failure of the Liberal Party to adopt policies which could appeal to working men was not wholly due to the Liberal leadership: the Liberal rank-and-file were also to blame. For another consequence of the secession of the Liberal Unionists in 1886 was to give the nonconformists and their radical allies a greater say in the formation of the party's policies – and this had two important consequences. It meant, first, the adoption by the party of nonconformist fads – local option, disestablishment in Wales and Scotland – in which the workers had no real interest, and which helped to account for the defeat of 1895 (**98**). It meant, second, that leading nonconformist employers – many of whom held key positions in the provincial party organisations – were often conspicuous for their anti-trade union attitudes and devotion to 'individualism' (**20**).

The suspicion of labour leaders for the Liberal caucus was, therefore, often confirmed; and this was further reinforced by the refusal of many local Liberal Associations to countenance working men as parliamentary candidates, as in the classic case of Keir Hardie at Mid-Lanark in 1888 [**doc. 29**]. The consequences of this were seen in the last five years of the nineteenth century. Then, on the one hand, the Liberal Party began to lose support to the Right – to a Conservative Party which through its superior organisation and built-in advantages could exploit successfully the disunity, weaknesses and sectarianism of the Liberals, and the grievances of the working class (**98, 109**). But it also began to lose support to the Left: for since in practice the Liberal Party did so little for them, a new generation of labour leaders were now determined to assert their political independence more forcibly. One way in which they could do this was by standing as Labour candidates in local elections, which they did with considerable success – at the expense of Liberalism – in areas like East London (**131**). It is indeed the disastrous withering of the local roots of Liberalism during the 'nineties that anticipates the national decline of the party in the twentieth century. Another way in which they could assert their independence was by forming their own national party. The foundation of the Labour Party in 1900, therefore, is a fitting comment on the failures of the Liberal Party in the age of Rosebery and Harcourt.

5 Conservative Domination

Conservatives and Liberal Unionists

The long period of Conservative ascendancy at the end of the nineteenth century is associated peculiarly with the powerful figure of Lord Salisbury, Prime Minister for nearly fourteen years between 1885 and his retirement in 1902. On becoming Prime Minister for the first time in June 1885 his major problem was the composition of the new ministry, and the clash of personalities among the contenders for office made it an especially delicate one. Two men were particulary important. On the one hand there was Sir Stafford Northcote who, despite the supine role he had played as Conservative Leader in the Commons in the previous five years, was a respected member of the party and a man of considerable ministerial experience: having been denied the highest post he wished at the very least to continue as Leader in the Commons. On the other hand there was Lord Randolph Churchill. Salisbury had already had one brush with him (as we saw earlier in our discussion of party organisation) over the National Union in 1883–84, and was acutely aware of the defects as well as the remarkable powers of this *enfant terrible* of the Conservative Party. Nevertheless, by 1885 Lord Randolph Churchill had proved himself the most formidable opponent of the Liberal Government both inside and outside the House of Commons – and one of the few Conservatives who could arouse working-class audiences. To attempt to form a Conservative Government 'without the man who is far and away the most popular Conservative in the House of Commons', as Hicks-Beach wrote to Salisbury, was an impossibility; and the Prime Minister perforce agreed (**61**, p. 176).

There was, however, one stumbling block – Churchill refused to serve under Northcote in the House of Commons. Since no Conservative Ministry could survive which did not contain both men, Salisbury had somehow or other to resolve their claims and those of their adherents, a task which was rendered particularly difficult by the vacillation of Northcote and the aloofness and arrogance of

Churchill. For some days there was an impasse while recriminations mounted within the party. Eventually, as a result of the patience, good sense and insight of Salisbury, Northcote was 'kicked upstairs' as the Earl of Iddesleigh and made First Lord of the Treasury; Lord Randolph Churchill accepted the India Office, and his protagonist, Michael Hicks-Beach, became Leader in the Commons and Chancellor of the Exchequer. 'What a triumph!', wrote Chamberlain to Churchill. 'You have won all along the line.' Superficially this appeared to be true. Lord Randolph had won high office at an early age – he was only thirty-five – and with no ministerial experience; and the leader of the 'old gang' had been forced virtually to commit political suicide. But the real victor was once again, as in 1884, the man who had, with consummate skill, imposed his will on the members of the Conservative front bench and thereby consolidated his leadership of the party. 'The successful formation of his first ministry', writes R. R. James, 'was the first and possibly the most important of the triumphs in domestic politics achieved by Lord Salisbury' (**61**, p. 189).

The methods adopted by Churchill to push himself into office did little to endear him to the more orthodox members of the Conservative Party; they grumbled and waited. But from a strictly ministerial point of view he was an undoubted success at the India Office, and this fact, together with his brilliant onslaught on Gladstone's Home Rule policy in 1886, meant that he was bound to be considered for promotion when Lord Salisbury, after the Unionist success at the polls in the summer of that year, came to form his second Ministry. Salisbury's doubts about Lord Randolph's temperamental fitness for Cabinet office and his suspicions of 'Tory Democracy' did not make him relish the prospect; nevertheless, once Hicks-Beach had insisted on yielding his place to him, there was no alternative but to appoint him Leader of the House and Chancellor of the Exchequer. 'He is very able', wrote Lord Cranbrook, 'but has he the balanced mind, the control of temper, the ready judgement, the knowledge of the House, of friends, of foes, which are requisite for a leader?' (**61**, p. 250). Within a few months these doubts seemed to be confirmed. It was not only that Lord Randolph insisted on treating the Prime Minister as a political equal; nor was it just his promulgation of Tory Democracy to the country at large behind the back of the Cabinet – as in his notorious Dartford Speech in October 1886 – and his intimate political friendship with Joseph Chamberlain, still a dangerous radical in the eyes of orthodox Conservatives. Rather it was, in Salisbury's own phrase, his 'incessant interference' and his attempt to impose his own policies on the Cabinet that was his most heinous offence; and this was particularly true of the Chancellor's brash attempts to influence the Government's foreign policy – always Salisbury's first interest – now in the hands of his old opponent, Lord Iddesleigh.

By November Churchill was at odds with most of his colleagues over practically every aspect of policy – Ireland, local government, procedural reform as well as foreign affairs; and though Salisbury deferred to him as much as he could, his patience was wearing thin, as shown clearly in his letter to Cranbrook [**doc. 30**]. It was at this point, as his daughter suggests, that Salisbury came to the conclusion that the point of no return had been reached in his relationship with Churchill: 'The experiment had failed . . . a breach was inevitable.' It is against this background of Salisbury's mounting irritation and Lord Randolph's increasing sense of isolation and frustration, that we must see the latter's famous 'resignation' letter of 20 December 1886, which was promptly accepted by the Prime Minister (**61**, ch. x).

The immediate result of Churchill's resignation was a political crisis owing to the difficulty of filling the posts he had vacated. 'I take a very dark view of our future', wrote Balfour, 'I think we must break up.' This could only be avoided, Salisbury believed, if the Liberal Unionists, who had given the Government general support since its inception, now offered more positive help. It is at this point, therefore, that we may turn aside to consider the position of the small but vitally important group of Liberal Unionists led by that strange pair of bedfellows, Lord Hartington and Joseph Chamberlain.

The position of the Liberal Unionists after the general election of July 1886 depended on the simple fact that, partly as a result of their electoral pact with the Conservatives, they controlled seventy-eight votes in the House of Commons. This meant that the Conservative Government under Lord Salisbury was indirectly dependent on their support, for if they switched their votes to the official Liberal Party and the Irish, the Government must collapse. In this anomalous situation lay at once the strength of the Liberal Unionist Party – since in return for their support they could hope to obtain 'liberal' concessions from their Conservative allies – but also their weakness, since, so long as the Liberal Party under Gladstone with its commitment to Home Rule was the greater evil, they would be prepared in the last resort to prop up a Conservative Government whatever domestic policies it pursued, in order to maintain the Unionist front. The Liberal Unionists were in fact (like all third parties in British politics) in a cruel position. They had somehow or other, while giving general support to the Conservatives, to convince the country they were still *Liberals*; a confidence trick which in the end – as their connection with the parent party receded and the gravitational pull of the Conservative Party became more powerful – they found impossible to sustain. The point was put with admirable clarity by Joseph Chamberlain himself, writing to Hartington:

> Our great difficulty is that in order to preserve the Union we are forced to keep the Tory government in power. But every time we vote with them we give a shock to the ordinary Liberal politician outside, and if we do it too often, we shall be completely identified with the Tories and shall lose all chance of recovering the lead of the Liberal party' (**26**, ii, 268).

The problem was even more complex and difficult than this indicates since the Liberal Unionists were not even a united party. In effect, they consisted of a large group of about fifty moderates or Whigs who looked to Hartington as their leader, and a smaller group of radical unionists who followed Joseph Chamberlain; and the two leaders were now no more united over policy and tactics than they had been under Gladstone (**84**). Hartington neither saw the position of the Liberal Unionists in quite the way that Chamberlain did, nor worried over it unduly. He was a Unionist first and foremost; and, never a great reformer even in his Gladstonian days, his attitude towards many of the problems of the day was now even less progressive than many members of the Conservative front bench. Having refused the premiership in July 1886 on the reasonable grounds that it would worsen the general Unionist position by driving many Liberals back to Gladstone; freed at last from the spur of the G.O.M.'s personal presence, and bound in any case soon to succeed to the duchy of Devonshire, both temperament and conviction made Hartington content on the whole to cede the initiative to the Conservative leaders and demand little in return. It was an attitude which infuriated Chamberlain. 'It is', as he kept reiterating to him, 'a negative policy.' But in any case Salisbury's magnanimous offer of agreeing to serve under Hartington as Premier, and the fact that the latter controlled the bulk of the Liberal Unionists, created a false impression of Hartington's strength and that of his group. His passive leadership, and the moderateness of his supporters – 'so moderate', as a contemporary wrote, 'that a political microscope would have been necessary to distinguish them from Conservatives born and bred' (**84**, p. 72) – meant that they could provide the Conservative Party, as Akers-Douglas, the Conservative Chief Whip, shrewdly noted, with 'debating power in the House but outside their influence is more likely to be a source of weakness than strength' (**66**, p. 104). The moderates provided the shadow rather than the substance of Liberal Unionist power.

Far different was the position of Joseph Chamberlain. He had taken great pains right from the start to dissociate his brand of Unionism from that both of the Conservatives and the Whigs. He had, for example, in June 1886 issued his own independent election address, and in the same month formed the National Radical Union (even though most of its members also joined the Liberal Unionist Party); nor had he ever seriously considered the possibility of joining a Conservative-dominated Government. Chamberlain could afford to be independent. For, unlike Hartington, his real power lay not in Parliament, where he controlled only some twenty members, but, as M. C. Hurst has argued, in his electoral base in the Midlands: it was the 'rock of regionalism' that sustained him (**82**). His personal control for the Unionist cause of the great bloc of constituencies in and around Birmingham, made him both a local and a national figure of importance – and a powerful independent force in his own right. Though a passionate Unionist, Chamberlain intended, therefore, to use this power to push upon the Conservative Government a programme of reforms for Ireland and England; a policy which in his eyes had not only political but tactical merits. For Chamberlain had to prove that he was still a Liberal; not only to maintain the devotion of his Midlands supporters, and prevent the drift of Liberal Unionists – under the impact of Conservative reaction – back to the old party; but to cover his own retreat if, as he still believed possible, Gladstone retired, the Liberal Party dropped Home Rule, and a reunited party looked around for a new leader. The policy he tried to pursue, therefore, in the second half of 1886 was, as he suggested to Hartington, 'never to vote with the Tories unless they are in danger and to vote against them whenever we can safely do so' (**26**, ii, 268). This was the attitude he adopted, though with considerable difficulty, towards the Government's Irish policy, while at the same time he tried to influence it, mainly through Lord Randolph Churchill, in the direction of more liberal policies generally.

It was this policy of vicarious Liberalism that seemed to be struck a vigorous blow by the resignation of Churchill in December

1886. 'I interpreted the event', wrote Chamberlain, 'as meaning that the reactionary party in the Cabinet had gained the upper hand' (**27**, p. 233). One important result of this was an attempt at Liberal reunion, on the initiative of Chamberlain and Harcourt, in the 'Round Table Conference' early in 1887. It was an odd episode. The bitterness between the two sides, the absence of Gladstone and Hartington – let alone the Irish – from the discussions, the continuance of mutual recriminations even while the conference was sitting, gave it an air of unreality and made its failure almost a foregone conclusion. In fact, it has been argued, in a detailed study by Mr Hurst, that Chamberlain's motives in supporting the conference were purely tactical. It was not a real attempt at reunion but a gesture towards his Birmingham supporters to show that his heart was still in the right place and that he had not gone over to the Conservatives unconditionally; just as he could argue once the conference was broken off that it was Gladstone and not he who was preventing reunion (**83**).

The resignation of Lord Randolph Churchill, however, as we have already seen, had another effect as far as the Liberal Unionists were concerned: it made the Conservatives more dependent on them for ministerial support. Indeed, Salisbury went so far as to offer the premiership once again to Hartington; but though he refused, for reasons similar to those that had moved him in July, he did strongly support the appointment of Goschen, the Liberal Unionists' financial expert, as Chancellor, although without committing the party as a whole. Goschen's appointment at the beginning of 1887, together with the unexpected choice of W. H. Smith as Leader of the House and A. J. Balfour as Irish Secretary (both as it turned out excellent appointments) ended successfully the political crisis that had faced Salisbury since the end of 1886.

Eighteen eighty-seven thus marks something of a turning point in the history of the Liberal Unionist Party, and its position after that date is described clearly by Joseph Chamberlain in his *Political Memoir* [**doc. 31**]. For him too it was to be an important year. It seemed impossible to go back. 'I am reluctantly forced to the conclusion', he said at Birmingham in 1887, 'that the cleavage in the ranks of the Liberal Party has become complete and irretrievable' (**26**, ii, 310); and it was hopeless to attempt to form a new party, especially as soon very few Liberal Associations were left to the Liberal Unionists. The only thing to do was to go forward – towards the Conservative Party, which at least offered the possibility of eventual office, and to a man of Chamberlain's energy and ability this was an important consideration. In 1887 he accepted from Lord Salisbury the leadership of a small delegation to the United States to discuss a fisheries dispute – a trivial incident, but the thin end of the wedge perhaps.

It was not just personal ambition, however, that made Chamberlain move inexorably towards the Conservative Party; changing political and economic circumstances were even more important. For if Chamberlain needed the Conservative Party, they also in a sense needed him: as a Midland political 'boss', and as a radical who could act as a Unionist spokesman to the working class. A new *rapport* was now particularly urgent since the Government's majority was steadily dropping owing to the loss of by-elections to the Liberals; it was, therefore, bound to take more heed of the Chamberlainite reform programme, especially too as Churchill was now in the political wilderness. 'His influence accumulates though his party decays', wrote the parliamentary commentator, Henry Lucy; and Chamberlain was well aware of this. In 1889 he wrote to Hartington: 'We want to convince the country that there is a better chance of really popular reform from a Unionist Government than from the Parnell–Gladstone. It is true that certain great changes desired by many Liberals and by all Radicals are out of the question. Disestablishment is one of these' (**84**).

Thus, though in the course of the next few years Chamberlain more or less abandoned his nonconformist past and the reform programme associated with it, he came to convince himself that the Salisbury Ministry – with its reforms in local government, landholding, Ireland, and education – was a genuine reformist government, introducing in fact much of his own 1885 'Unauthorised Programme'. It was these 'popular' reforms passed by a Conservative ministry under his influence, that he could now contrast with the irrelevant absurdities of the Liberal 'Newcastle Programme' of 1891, an attempt, as he said, 'to harmonise the political economy of Mr Tom Mann and Mr John Morley' (**26**, ii, 520).

Though it would be false to denigrate Chamberlain's genuine and continuing interest in social reform during the years after 1887, it is clear nevertheless that his mind was turning more and more towards imperial affairs, and here his sympathies were even more with the policies of Lord Salisbury than they were with the 'Little Englandism' of the predominant section of the Liberal Party. In 1889 he strongly supported the Government's retention of Egypt, and in the same year he visited the country and vigorously defended England's policies there in a speech at Birmingham in 1890.

'From that moment', says Garvin, 'he stood out as the leader of the new Imperialism', and Salisbury's work in Africa in the course of the next few years received his warm support. This new mutual respect between Chamberlain and the Conservative leaders was increased when in 1891 Hartington retired to the Lords as the eighth Duke of Devonshire and Chamberlain became leader of the Liberal Unionists in the Commons, for he was able to establish particularly friendly relations with A. J. Balfour who became Conservative Leader there in the same year. Thus, symbolically, towards the end of 1891 Chamberlain sat side by side with Salisbury at a meeting in Birmingham of the Conservative National Union and declared the Unionist alliance 'indissoluble': 'Now', he said, referring to the Liberals, 'I neither look for nor desire reunion' (**26**, ii, 443).

One last factor remained, that was finally to push Chamberlain and the Liberal Unionists towards a real alliance with the Conservative Party, and that was the record of the Liberal Government between 1892 and 1895. It was not only that, for Chamberlain, the Liberals were tied indissolubly to the Irish Party and still committed to Home Rule; it was their attacks on the House of Lords which he particularly resented, for he saw them as an attempt to get round the fact that the English people had supported the Lords' rejection of the Second Home Rule Bill in 1893. But, at a more profound level, he also linked the 'new Liberalism' of the 'Newcastle Programme' and the attacks on the Lords with the growing menace of Socialism, a menace which was encouraged not only by these policies but by the weakness and disunity of the Liberal Party itself. A spectre was haunting England in the 1890s, in Chamberlain's imagination, the spectre of Socialism; and it was essential for all supporters of private property rights to sink their smaller differences in the face of this larger menace [**doc. 32**]. Thus, as Peter Fraser writes, 'the socialist threat to property that emerged in the course of the Liberal ministries of 1892–95 provided just the tide of opinion that Chamberlain wanted to carry his party across the floor' (**80**). Hence in 1894 Chamberlain spoke on behalf of the Conservatives, and both sides began to think seriously about the implications of a Unionist victory at the next general election.

Chamberlain and the Liberal Unionists obtained from Salisbury much of what they wanted, and the sweeping Unionist victory in 1895 led Chamberlain, Devonshire and other Liberal Unionists to join Salisbury's third ministry, thus making it, in Ensor's phrase, 'one of the strongest that has ever held office in Great Britain' (**2**). The independent Liberal Unionist organisation, however, still remained, for as Chamberlain wrote somewhat petulantly to Devonshire: 'the rank and file in the country still maintain many of the old prejudices and will not join a Conservative party or Conservative organisation' (**80**). The Unionist Party after 1895 was thus essentially a coalition: but a coalition united to defend not only the Union but propertied interests generally.

The basis of Conservative power

Despite the remarkable change that took place in the leadership of the Conservative Party between the 1870s and the 1890s, there was little fundamental change in the character of the party or the nature of its support. The swing of the middle-class voter to the right which (as has been argued above) was typical of the age of Disraeli, was accelerated rather than halted in the age of the aristocratic Cecils; and, in particular, the leaders of financial and commercial wealth – formerly Liberal – were coming to find their natural resting place more and more in the party of Salisbury and Chamberlain. Ensor, in a much quoted article, argued that the primary cause of this metamorphosis was Irish crime and violence – itself the consequence, fundamentally, of the agricultural depression which hit both Ireland and England after 1873 (**119**). This view is really far too simple; for the changes in political allegiance which he discusses arose out of the general 'liberalisation' of mid-Victorian society and the rise of the working class. Nevertheless, Ensor does well to draw our attention to the importance of Irish affairs and agricultural depression in explaining the political displacements that occurred in the later nineteenth century. For if the Irish troubles of the 'eighties did not cause, they at least stimulated the exodus of businessmen from the Liberal to the Conservative Party; and, as historians from Halévy onwards have noted, the Liberal Unionist Party which emerged as a result of the Home Rule crisis of 1886 was in a real sense the political expression of their economic power (**3, 81**).

The importance of the agricultural depression is perhaps even greater in considering the long-term development of the Conservative Party. For in the 'seventies and 'eighties it did help to undermine the economic position of at least an important section of the landed classes – the backbone of Conservatism – and thus revealed all too clearly their inability to pretend that they controlled any longer the real keys of political and administrative power. The decline of the landed interest in the later nineteenth century – psychological perhaps even more than economic – made it inevitable that the Conservative Party should accept for its own good the blood transfusion of energy, ability and, above all, wealth that the middle-class plutocracy could provide. In any case, as F. M. L. Thompson has shown, the distinction between 'landed' and 'commercial' wealth was rapidly becoming a myth, at least for the upper echelons of landed society, whose members, like the Dukes of Devonshire and Northumberland, and even Salisbury himself, were now investing widely in industrial and railway shares and commercial ventures overseas (**116**). After 1886, therefore, the Conservative Party was well on the way to becoming the party of the landed and financial plutocracy, and mainly responsible for that 'atmosphere of money in the lobby of the House of Commons' that the *Economist* found so reprehensible in 1899 (**3**, p. 17). From this point of view, too, the political alliance of 1895 between the Conservative and Liberal Unionist parties was merely the parliamentary expression of an economic and social *fait accompli* which had been building up during the previous thirty years.

The Conservative Party in the later years of the nineteenth century, therefore, was no longer dominated completely by the ethos of the landed classes (with whom may be associated the Church of England), but by the interests of the propertied classes generally; and this is reflected to some extent in the composition of both houses of Parliament. Here, as in so many other ways, the year 1885 is something of a turning point. For after the general election of that year for the first time members of the industrial and commercial interest outnumbered members of the landed interest in the House of Commons. This was, of course, merely the middle class coming belatedly into its parliamentary inheritance, as Bagehot had already noted in 1872 in one of the most famous sections of his *English Constitution* (**10**, p. 274). But since the Liberal Party had nearly twice as many commercial as landed men in the House of Commons as early as 1868, it is the changes in the parliamentary composition of the Conservative Party after that date that are the more remarkable; though these, it must be admitted, are difficult to assess precisely, owing to the problems of defining the different 'groups'. But in 1868, according to the figures of W. L. Guttsman, 46 per cent of Conservative M.P.s belonged to the landed interest; 31 per cent came from commerce and industry; and 9 per cent belonged to the professions. In 1885 the figures for these three groups were 23 per cent, 50 per cent and 16 per cent respectively; and in 1900 (including Liberal Unionists) 20, 52 and 18 per cent (**122**,

p. 104). This would indicate a fairly rapid fall in the numbers belonging to the landed interest (but see **64**).

Another, slighter, indication of the change in the character of the Conservative Party can be seen in the membership of the Upper House. 'Tradition, personal merit, and Bagehot's plutocracy made terms with one another', writes F. M. L. Thompson, 'and nowhere is this more visible than in the history of the peerage after 1885' (**116**, p. 292). The number of peerages themselves rose after that date; but what is more significant is the increasing ennoblement of those with commercial and industrial backgrounds. In the ten years before 1886 only four such peerages had been created, in the ten years after 1886 there were eighteen; and in the whole period from 1886 to 1914 out of the 200 or so men who then entered the peerage for the first time, more than a third were industrialists and less than a quarter were members of landed families (**116, 121**). The turning point in this process, writes its historian, 'appears to have been ... the first Salisbury ministry in 1885–86' when 'for the first time, and always thereafter, 20 per cent or more of all recipients had [commercial and industrial] connections' (**120**); a tribute in itself to the Prime Minister's recognition of party needs. One other indication perhaps of the changing nature of the Conservative Party is the rise of the Fair Trade Movement after 1881 and its close links with the party. It is true, of course, that a section of the farmers (though not the greater landowners) strongly supported the movement and reflected, therefore, the traditional link between the Conservative Party and the land. But, as the historian of the League suggests, the spread of its ideas 'was largely the work of manufacturers who suffered from foreign competition and foreign tariffs' (**118**, p. 1); and the fact, therefore, that at least six members of Salisbury's Government in 1886 spoke favourably of its ideas, and that the Conservative National Union in 1887 and 1891 carried protectionist motions, is an indication now of the party's increasing concern for the interests of trade and industry rather than of agriculture. It reveals too the key importance of the views of the small group of Conservative members who sat for industrial constituencies in Sheffield, Bradford, and elsewhere, where industry was hard hit by increasing competition from abroad.

It would be completely false to assume, however, that these changes in the composition of the Parliamentary Conservative Party were reflected proportionately in its leadership. In fact, as is clear purely from *prima facie* evidence, the leaders of Conservative governments and the party machine were still mainly aristocratic or associated with the landed interest: what is more remarkable, therefore, about the Conservative Party in the later nineteenth century is not the decline of the landed interest in terms of wealth and numbers, which was inevitable, but the tenacity and relative ease with which it was able to cling to its over-representation in every aspect of party life. This was of course a tribute to the ability of a Salisbury, an Akers-Douglas or an A. J. Balfour; but, Cornford adds, ability decided 'only which aristocrats should dominate the party' (**64**). How far this was an electoral asset in an age when, Halévy suggests, the peerage was particularly popular, is difficult to determine (**3**, p. 22). But what does seem beyond dispute is that the partnership of wealth *and* title within the ranks of the Unionist Party did give it considerable advantages. It helps to explain the success of Conservative organisation compared with the Liberals; for it was money that helped to oil the wheels of the efficient party machine controlled by Akers-Douglas and Capt. Middleton and enabled them, for example, to employ thirty party agents in the London area to the Liberals' three (**131**, p. 110). This was particularly important in the great cities where the Conservative Party was appealing successfully to the working classes. In the rural areas such overt organisation was hardly necessary. The county *élite* of farmers, gentry and Anglican clergy – stolidly Unionist after 1886, and still dominating the bench and local government – exercised a real, though unacknowledged, 'pull' over the local voters in favour of the Conservative Party, and made the task of the Liberal worker in most country constituencies particularly heartbreaking (**98, 105**).

The Conservative Party also gained from the inbuilt advantages that the electoral system itself gave to owners of property. For, contrary to popular belief, the electoral legislation of the 1880s did not, as Charles Seymour pointed out half a century ago, introduce 'a completely democratic system', even apart from the obvious fact that women did not possess the vote (**102**, p. 156); and in his detailed study of the franchise system between 1885 and 1918 Neal Blewett has shown that something like 40 per cent of adult males did not exercise the vote (**107**). Why was this? Some men were in fact specifically excluded from the franchise: domestic servants, policemen and soldiers living in barracks, and – particularly resented – those on poor relief. But even more damning was the fact that about half of those who were not on the electoral register in 1911 were excluded, not because they lacked the necessary franchise qualifications, but through the workings of the archaic registration system, with its insistence, for example, on twelve months' possession to exercise the household franchise. This great army of the disenfranchised-in-practice – about one million men annually – consisted mainly of working men, often changing jobs, and it is impossible to tell exactly how they would have voted after 1885 if given the chance. But, by contrast, if the poor often lost the vote, the rich often gained votes owing to the practice by which owners of businesses and university graduates were given votes additional to the ones they exercised in their home constituencies. Such plural votes, it has been estimated, amounted (in 1911) to some 7 per cent of the total electorate (**107**); and though we may discount the wilder claims made by Opposition spokesmen in the 'nineties in denouncing the system of plural voting, both Seymour and Blewett conclude that it did produce some bias in favour of the Unionists.

They gained even more from the Redistribution Act of 1885 which they insisted – owing to the successful Conservative black-mailing tactics in the House of Lords – should accompany the Reform Act of the previous year (**111**). For the Conservative Party was alarmed lest the considerable increase in votes produced by that Act – the number of voters rose from about 900,000 to 2½ million in the counties – should, if unaccompanied by redistribution, swamp the old constituencies and produce an overwhelming swing to the left. Hence, paradoxically, the Conservative leadership was prepared to support a radical redistribution measure which would sacrifice the small boroughs in favour of an almost universal division of the country into one-member constituencies; believing that, however the rural labourer voted, the Conservative Party would still make great gains in the cities. 'I believe there is', commented Salisbury, 'a great deal of villa Toryism which requires organisation.' Roughly speaking that is what did happen. The abolition or reduction of the representation of the smaller boroughs by the 1885 Act made 142 seats available for redistribution: sixty-eight were given to the English and Welsh counties, but seventy-four went to the boroughs, with the great provincial cities gaining three to six more members and Greater London gaining another thirty-nine (**102**). The country was at the same time divided up into constituencies roughly equal in population; and the parliamentary map of Great Britain which had existed without fundamental change for some three centuries finally disappeared, unmourned (**108**). The position in the cities was now vital. They were carved up deliberately on largely 'class' lines, and the importance of this fact for the Conservative Party is put succinctly by Professor Cornford: 'Where

Conservative supporters had formerly been swamped in huge constituencies, they were now high and dry on islands of their own'
(**63**). The result of this was seen in 1885 when for the first time the
Conservatives won a majority in the English boroughs. Indeed the
pattern laid down in that election – when Conservative strength
was concentrated in London, Lancashire, the non-industrial counties, and the smallest and largest of the boroughs – was to be
roughly repeated in the next five elections (**63**).

So far we have considered certain general advantages possessed
by the Conservative Party in the later nineteenth century. What,
however, was the role of Conservative leadership and policy in
accounting for the party's long period of domination? Lord Salisbury, who led the Conservative Party during the years between
1885 and 1902, was in some ways, despite his outstanding qualities
as a statesman, an odd person to be party leader during this period
(**69, 76**). He himself, as he said, lacked 'the gifts of pliancy and
optimism' (**68**, iii, 110) which he believed the leader of a great party must possess; and his agility of mind, mordant wit, and political
cynicism, were often disconcerting to his slower colleagues. 'He
was', as Paul Smith suggests, 'one of those untypical and sometimes uncongenial figures, like Peel, or Disraeli, or Churchill, by
whom the Conservative party allows itself to be led from time to
time, because it needs the qualities of intellect, or imagination, or
character which they can supply' (**75**, intro.).

In a profound sense he was never really a politician in the way
that Disraeli was, just as he totally lacked his predecessor's flair for
publicity; but, though he despised such things, he did what was required of him by way of dispensing patronage and stumping the
country. He ran the Cabinet on a very loose reign, and much pre-
ferred the Foreign Office to being Prime Minister, a post which, he
remarked, conferred 'no real power' (**68**, iii, 111). At the Foreign
Office, of course, his work was outstanding; in domestic affairs,
however, he possessed, suggests A. J. P. Taylor, 'the outlook of a
slow-witted countryman'. This is perhaps going a bit far, though
Salisbury would have relished the remark. But certainly the Prime
Minister's brand of Conservatism, with its emphasis on the need for
individual effort and strong government and its barely concealed
distaste for state activity, democracy and progress, seemed to belong to a bygone age (**78**). 'I reckon myself', he wrote, 'as no higher
in the state of things than a policeman – whose utility would be
gone if the workers of mischief disappeared' (**68**, iii, 147). He
tended perhaps to see 'workers of mischief' all around him on the

domestic front in the 1890s, and his correspondence is full of gloomy forebodings for the future. Such an outlook, together with a penchant for giving jobs to his relatives, led to grumblings from those more progressive Conservative members – such as J. A. Gorst or G. C. T. Bartley – who felt that they were outside the magic circle [**doc. 33**]. But Salisbury's power, in a strictly party sense, rested securely on the support of the landed classes, and on the lucky fact that, on the outstanding issues of the day – Ireland, Socialism, foreign and imperial policy – his views coincided with those of the overwhelming majority of Conservative members. His nephew and successor, A. J. Balfour, was not to be so lucky.

It was hardly to be expected then that Salisbury would prove to be a great reformer. 'He was', writes his daughter, 'by temperament and opinion incapable of becoming a great law-maker. He did not believe in any good to be affected by "inspired" ventures in legislation' (**68**, iii, 167). He was not averse to some aspects of reform, as in housing or local government; and, as he observed cynically of the County Councils Bill of 1888, it was in the fashion, and 'against fashion it is almost impossible to argue' (**59**, p. 142). But his attitude towards reform was conditioned less by his personal predilections, than by his understanding of the character of the Conservative Party, the pulls and pressures of groups, interests and individuals within it, and the situation in which it found itself after 1886; in all of which he was powerfully helped by the support and advice of Akers-Douglas and Capt. Middleton, Chief Whip and party agent. For, in the first place, Lord Salisbury was conscious – over-conscious some loyal supporters believed in 1886 – of the vital importance of Liberal Unionist support; and was realistic enough to realise that some reform was needed to placate it. 'It is the price we have to pay for the Union', he wrote of the Irish Land Bill of 1887, 'and it is a heavy one' (**65**). But it was a price he was always prepared to pay (**70**). As Peter Marsh argues, 'Opposition to Home Rule was the keystone of Salisbury's power', and it is this that helps to explain also his strong support for Balfour's tough policy in Ireland during the years of his Secretaryship, and his hounding of Parnell over the '*Times* Forgeries' in 1887 (**73**).

Part of that price also, more negatively, was the inability of the party to abandon Free Trade in the 'eighties and early 'nineties, and it is his awareness of that basic limitation that explains Salisbury's hedging over the issue when confronted with the protectionist sentiments of the Conservative National Union (**118**). Quite apart from the alliance with the Liberal Unionists, however, as Cornford observes 'the Conservative party itself was a coalition, both socially and politically' (**64**). This meant that the Prime Minister had to face pressure also from the 'reformist' group of M.P.s within the party, many of whom sat for industrial constituencies and who were, therefore, forced to push the interests of their working-class constituents. It was these men who, as we have seen, often supported the protectionist movements of the period; and it was they also who were most sympathetic to the Chamberlainite proposals for social reform, like the scheme for old age pensions.

For a variety of reasons, then, Salisbury was willing to accept a number of reforms, some of which went against the grain; and on occasion he was prepared to use blackmail tactics to impose them upon his recalcitrant right wing. But there was a limit to what he could or would do, and that limit was set, he believed, and as he pointed out in a remarkable letter to Lord Randolph Churchill, by the attitudes of 'the classes and the dependants of class', the country gentlemen and their supporters [**doc. 34**]. For in Salisbury's eyes they still formed the most important section of the Conservative Party: the most stable, the most worthy and the most loyal, and indeed the group with whom his real sympathies lay. It was their interests, their prejudices even, that must be taken into account when considering the programme of the party. Not that he did much for them positively. 'They will not find – they cannot find', he wrote, in reference to the agricultural depression, 'in the doctrines of protection any alleviation from the ruin which in too many instances threatens them' (**68**, iv, 180 1). But it was of them he was probably thinking when he wrote of the Conservative Party in a valedictory letter to Alfred Milner:

> It is a party shackled by tradition; all the cautious people, all the timid, all the unimaginative, belong to it. It stumbles slowly and painfully from precedent to precedent with its eyes fixed on the ground. Yet the Conservative Party is the Imperial Party. I must work with it – who indeed am just such an one myself... (**65**).

Conservative reform legislation (or lack of it) was often the outcome of subtle and detailed negotiations and conflict within the party. But when all is said and done it cannot be maintained that the party's record was very impressive during the fourteen or so years of Salisbury's rule. One great Act – the County Councils Act of 1888 – and a few minor ones were passed during his second ministry between 1886 and 1892; after 1895, even with Chamberlain and the Liberal Unionists in the Government, the record was even thinner; and over the whole period of Salisbury's ascendancy practically nothing was done to improve the condition of life of the working classes. Why was this? And why was the Conservative Party able to maintain itself in power during this long period?

The orthodox answer usually given by historians is that the masses were beguiled by imperialism. Professor Beer, in his book on *Modern British Politics*, puts the argument quite unequivocally. The lack of social reform, he writes, 'is most readily explained on simple electoral grounds. In imperialism (including in this not only the question of Empire but also of union with Ireland) the party had found a cause with a mighty appeal to the electorate' (**90**, p. 272). But if the general trend of much recent research on later nineteenth-century political history has been, by implication, to cast doubt on the view that (except in special areas like Lancashire) the working-class electorate was vitally influenced by the Home Rule issue, the same point has been made by Henry Pelling about imperialism proper. 'There is no evidence', he writes, 'of a direct continuous support for the cause of Imperialism among any section of the working class' (**128**, p. 99). The rhetoric of imperialism in its Kiplingesque aspect, he argues, never appealed to the working class at all. The only election during this period where imperial sentiment played a part was the notorious 'Khaki Election' of 1900, where it probably helped to stave off a Liberal victory (the Government's majority had been falling rapidly); though even there he stresses the importance of social and economic factors. In 1895, where Ensor sees the Unionist victory as due primarily to the force of 'expansive imperialism', Pelling emphasises economic factors and the unpopularity of Liberal policies (**2, 128**).

Pelling's views have now been reinforced by Richard Price's detailed study of the working class and the Boer War, based on evidence mainly from the working-men's clubs. He too finds an absence of jingoism, almost an indifference to the war, and indeed the existence in an inchoate and unorganised fashion of strong anti-war feeling (**133**). Imperialism for the working class was primarily important from the point of view of jobs and wages; and (as Pelling argues elsewhere) they were not in any case much interested in social reform *per se* – that was the prerogative of middle-class do-gooders (**128**, ch. 1). Perhaps, therefore, this 'jobs' aspect of imperialism did have some effect during the later 'nineties: not Salisbury's view that the scramble for Africa was 'a great civilising, Christianising force' (**68**, iv, 310), but rather his argument that 'to keep our trade, our industries alive we must open new sources of consumption in the more untrodden portions of the earth' (**59**, p. 106). But certainly, whatever its effect on the working class, such an appeal was bound to tie the forces of industrial and commercial wealth ever more closely to the Conservative Party.

Two general conclusions may, therefore, be tentatively suggested to account for Conservative domination in the later nineteenth century. First, it was not so much that the mass of voters were attracted positively to Conservative policies and politicians, but rather that they reacted against the weaknesses of contemporary Liberalism. This is linked to some extent with the 'lull' in political fervour that Professor Hanham notes as characteristic of this period (**86**, p. 27), and is shown in working-class abstentions at the polls. Secondly, working-class voters were concerned primarily with bread-and-butter issues – jobs, wages, prices – often seen within a specifically local context, as with the issue of immigration in East London in 1900 (**100, 131**). It was the link between these issues and their 'image' of the parties, that explained how and whether they voted. But these are almost guesses until we know more about the 'sociology' of elections in the constituencies during this period.

Part Three: Assessment

At the death of Queen Victoria in 1901 the British party system
was already beginning to assume the shape that it was to retain until at least the outbreak of the Second World War. The Conservative Party, as a result of the developments in the later nineteenth
century that have already been discussed, had, by that date, man-
aged to build up a firm electoral base by winning the allegiance of
the bulk of the middle class, and obtaining normally about one-
third of the working-class vote. It was the ability of the Conservative Party to gain the support of such a large section of the working
class that has enabled it since 1885 to win a clear majority of the
general elections that have been held, and thus to exhibit, in the
words of McKenzie and Silver, 'a record of electoral success almost
unrivalled among political parties in parliamentary systems' (**130**,
p. 10). Yet, curiously, the Conservative Party in 1901, though dependent on mass support, was led by that epitome of the old aristocratic ruling class, the Marquis of Salisbury; and, after Salisbury's
retirement in 1902, he was succeeded for another nine years by
another Cecil, his nephew, A. J. Balfour.

Yet appearances are deceptive. The political foundations of the
'Hotel Cecil' were being undermined well before Balfour was forced
to retire as leader of the party in 1911. For in a party which was
becoming increasingly dominated financially, and at the parliamentary level, by businessmen, it was impossible to stave off for
ever the evil day when they would demand some return, in terms of
real leadership, for their support. Deference might still be shown to
the aristocracy; but that deference was now based not on blood and
title but on political skill and success. And those were the very
things that Balfour was unable to provide. The ease with which he
had slipped into the premiership in 1902 after his uncle's retirement was a tribute, not so much to Balfour's family name, as to the
ability he had displayed earlier as Irish Secretary and Leader of the
Commons. Unfortunately, his behaviour after that date showed
that he lacked the qualities of firmness and decisiveness necessary
in a Prime Minister, and possessed, moreover, an olympian insensi-

tiveness to powerful currents of opinion both in the country – as shown by his egregious blunder over 'Chinese slavery' – and indeed within his own party, though this was partly due to the tameness of the National Union. Hence within eighteen months of becoming Prime Minister Balfour was faced with a crisis over tariff reform precipitated by Joseph Chamberlain; and, though he desperately tried to maintain his own supremacy and heal the fissures in the party, he eventually gave up the attempt and resigned as Prime Minister in 1905 (**26**, vols v and vi). The colossal electoral disaster of 1906, together with – as many Conservative back-benchers came to feel – his subsequent puerile leadership during the constitutional crises of 1909–11, led to a 'Balfour must go' movement; and in November 1911 he resigned as leader of the Conservative Party.

The replacement of Balfour by Bonar Law, the Scots-Canadian ironmaster, seemed to symbolise the coming to power within the party of the new type of Conservative industrialist. Law's successors, Baldwin and Neville Chamberlain, were men of much the same stamp; and the Conservative Party in the interwar years, therefore, seemed to be dominated by those 'hard-faced businessmen' who had begun to enter the party in the age of Disraeli. Nor did the change in the character of its leadership have any profound effect on the party's electoral position. It was the Conservative Party that gained most from the wartime coalition and the subsequent 'Coupon Election' of 1918; but the country was in any case moving to the right, and Conservative or Conservative-dominated governments were characteristic of the interwar period. Hence the Conservative Party, as so often in its long history, made a rapid recovery from the electoral defeats of 1906 and 1910. The Governments that were in power, therefore, between 1905 and 1914 proved to be not the first in a new cycle of Liberal ministries, but the 'last Liberal Governments of England'.

Why was this? The reasons for the decline of the Liberal Party have been much discussed recently by British historians (**54**). Since everyone agrees on the effects of the First World War in weakening the Liberal Party, our answer to the problem depends to a considerable extent on the view we take of the 1906 election, the Liberal Governments' achievements up to 1914, and the relationship between the Liberal and Labour Parties during the prewar period. Many historians and publicists, for example, though recognising many of the weaknesses of the Liberals that were apparent in the later Victorian period, have seen the great victory of 1906 as the beginning of a new period of Liberal revival which, based upon an

Assessment

increased working-class vote and the solid legislative achievements of the next six years, could have been sustained if it had not been for the disastrous divisions created by the First World War (**42**, **43**). This is roughly the argument of Trevor Wilson, who writes in his important book on the Liberal Party that 'if the party passed through troubled times between 1885 and 1905, its electoral victories from 1906 to 1910 appeared to show it fully recovered', though it is fair to add that his main purpose is to describe the period *after* 1914 (**38**, p. 18). But other historians have seen the success of the Liberals in 1906 as almost a gigantic fluke, the result of an exceptional concatenation of events; and, as far as the working class was concerned, the expression not of a profound demand for a 'new' Liberalism of increased state activity and social reform, but of a hankering after the old.

> The election [write Bealey and Pelling] was fought on the record of the Conservative Government and the fiscal proposals of Chamberlain: and it was the novel rather than the traditional elements of Conservatism that the voters condemned.... Imperialism, the new Education Act, Tariff Reform were all disavowed: the demand was for the return to nineteenth-century Gladstonianism, to the policies of Little England, to elected School Boards, and to Free trade... (**129**, p. 265).

The Liberal Party, therefore, in 1906 won on Gladstonian slogans and Gladstonian support: freetraders, nonconformists, the Irish and Little Englanders. But most of these groups were based on issues which were dead or dying: what neither 1906 nor its subsequent history up to 1914 revealed was a real determination on the part of the Liberal Party to overcome its long-term weaknesses, already apparent in the later nineteenth century. 'The recovery of the nineteen-hundreds', writes Paul Thompson, 'gave a deceptive illusion of strength, for it was not based on the solution of the Liberal Party's real problems. It still lacked a firm working-class basis, a secure financial backing and a coherent political standpoint. The test would come after defeat' (**131**, p. 189).

It was already perhaps too late. For there was one other factor whose long-term significance for the Liberal Party was to be even more decisive. In 1901, at the very end of our period, there were no longer two but three political parties in the state; and the Liberal Party was soon faced not only with the traditional rivalry of the Conservative Party, but the new and potentially even more dangerous rivalry of the Labour Party, founded in the previous year. It is true, of course, that during these prewar years the Liberal Party was able to 'contain' the Labour Party whose parliamentary membership never rose above forty-two (after the election of December 1910); and, as Trevor Wilson rightly points out, the impetus towards social reform during this decade comes from the Liberal rather than the Labour Party, (**38**, p. 19). Nevertheless, a number of labour historians have seen the long-term social and economic trends in the nation's development working for the Labour and against the Liberal party, and thus drawing the organised working class towards the former party (**128, 132**). The Parliamentary Labour Party may have been small during these years, but it was its growing extra-parliamentary support among the trade unions, so important in terms of membership, morale and finance, that was of decisive importance for the future. The Liberal Party had nothing comparable to fall back upon. It was the Labour Party, therefore, that became after 1918 the second party in the state.

Part Four: Documents

document 1

The nonconformists and the Liberal Party

The nonconformist community normally formed the most loyal bloc of voting support for the Liberal Party in the nineteenth century [but see **doc. 4**]. *The following extract well illustrates the reasons for this, and indicates also the 'tone' of much nonconformist writing on political affairs.*

Since the beginning of the century . . . it is certain that Britain has, in the intervals of her blindness, had some inspiring visions of the kingdom of justice one day to be established among men, and it is not to be denied that, taken broadly, the Liberal Party has striven to follow the fiery pillar of conscience into this promised land . . . speaking generally it has striven to be 'the party of Christ' . . . the party of moral principles as against that of selfish and corrupt interests, the party of peace as against that of violence, the party of popular improvement and reform as against that of resistance to progress, the party of justice as against that of despotic force or social disorder. . . . The strength of the Liberal Party is, and always has been, in the force of individual and social conscience.

From the *Nonconformist*, 1 January 1880 (quoted **20**).

document 2

Gladstone and the masses

Gladstone's Midlothian Campaign 1879–80 marked his re-entry into active politics, and was a bitter attack on Disraeli's foreign and imperial policies. The following extract shows why he was revered by the working people and distrusted by the upper classes.

'We have great forces arrayed against us. . . . I am sorry to say we cannot reckon upon what is called the landed interest, we cannot reckon upon the clergy of the established church either in England or Scotland. . . . On none of these can we place our trust. We cannot reckon on the wealth of the country, nor upon the rank of the country, nor upon the influence which rank and wealth usually bring. In the main these powers are against us, for wherever there is a close corporation, wherever there is a spirit of organised monopoly, wherever there is a narrow and sectional interest apart from that of the country, and desiring to be set up above the interest of the public, there, gentlemen, we, the liberal party, have no friendship and no tolerance to expect. Above all these, and behind all these, there is something greater than these – there is the nation itself.'

Speech at West Calder, 1 April 1880 (quoted **15**, ii, 218).

document 3
A Conservative view of the government, 1873

Northcote, like many leading Conservatives, supported Disraeli's refusal to take office in 1873 after Gladstone's temporary retirement. His letter reveals a remarkable understanding of the currents of opinion at work in the country.

But looking at the matter broadly, and in the interest of the Conservative cause as distinct from that of the present representatives of the Conservative party, I am strongly convinced that time is required to mature the fast ripening Conservatism of the country, and to dispel the hallucinations which have attached a great mass of moderate men to the Liberal cause. I believe that the disintegration of Gladstone's party has begun and that nothing but precipitancy on our part can arrest it. He has expended the impetuous force which brought him into office, and now is brought face to face with new, or rather old, difficulties which he can hardly surmount without alienating one or the other wing of his party. If he goes on with the Extreme section, a large body of his moderate supporters will rank themselves with the Conservatives, if he quarrels with the Extreme section they will become the Opposition, while the conduct of affairs will fall to the acknowledged Conservatives, who will obtain the support of the moderate Liberals. But if we appeal to the country before the breach in the Liberal ranks is fully made, and before the policy of the Extreme men is fully developed, we shall consolidate them; the Extreme men will hold back a little and the moderate advance a little and there will be more confusion and confiscation.

Sir Stafford Northcote to Disraeli, 14 March 1873 (quoted **99**, p. 14).

document 4
The nonconformist revolt

R. W. Dale was a Congregational minister and one of the leaders of the campaign against the Liberal Government's education policy.

They have deliberately chosen to pursue a retrograde policy, and although we have cherished a hearty loyalty to the old leaders of the Liberal Party, our loyalty to the principles which both they and we are called to defend is stronger, more intense, deeper than loyalty to them. We are at last thrown upon ourselves; for a time, perhaps, for a few years, we shall have to act independently of the recognised leaders of the Liberal party. The old union between them and us is now dissolved. I do not regard that dissolution with any degree of satisfaction.

From R. W. Dale, *The Elementary Education Act (1870) Amendment Bill and the Political Policy of Nonconformists*, Birmingham, 1873.

document 5
The decline of Gladstone's first ministry

Faced with opposition from nonconformists and working-men over his trade union and education Acts, and with weakness and disunity within the Cabinet, Gladstone hints at a dissolution and a new general election.

The signs of weakness multiply, and for some time have multiplied, upon the government, in the loss of control over the legislative action of the House of Lords, the diminution of the majority in the House of Commons without its natural compensation in increase of unity and discipline, and the almost unbroken series of defeats at single elections in the country. In truth the government is approaching, though I will not say it has yet reached, the condition in which it will have ceased to possess that amount of power which is necessary for the dignity of the crown and the welfare of the country; and in which it might be a godsend if some perfectly honourable difference of opinion among ourselves on a question requiring immediate action were to arise, and to take such a course as to release us collectively from the responsibilities of office...the nation appears to think that it has had enough of us....It is a question of measures then: can we by any measures materially mend the position of the party for an impending election?

Gladstone to Lord Granville, 8 January 1874 (quoted **15**, ii, 89–90).

document 6

The General Election of 1874

Frederic Harrison was a radical, a Positivist and a shrewd political analyst, as the following extract shows. The Fortnightly Review *was the leading highbrow radical journal of the mid-Victorian period, edited then by John Morley.*

The real truth is that the middle-class, or its effective strength, has swung round to Conservatism. Conservatism no doubt it is of a vague and negative kind; but its practical effect is an undefined preference for 'leaving well alone'. When we look at the poll in the City of London, in Westminster, in Middlesex, in Surrey, in Liverpool, Manchester, Leeds and Sheffield, in the metropolitan boroughs and in the home counties, in all the centres of middle-class industry, wealth and cultivation, we see one unmistakeable fact, that the rich trading-class, and the comfortable middle-class has grown distinctly Conservative. There are no special causes at work in these great constituencies. Beer has no influence with the merchants, shopkeepers and citizens of London. There are no dockyards in Surrey and Middlesex. There are no great landlords or employers in Marylebone. The Carlton Club cannot pull the wires of Manchester and Sheffield. The 25th Section men are not very strong in Westminster, and there is no 'residuum' in Hertfordshire and Essex, in Lancashire and Yorkshire counties. These great boroughs and counties contain the very flower of the men of business, whose indomitable energy builds up these five millions of surplus, who pay so large a proportion of that income-tax which was offered them as a bonus. The inference is unmistakeable. The effective force of the middle-class has grown for a season Conservative. The Conservative party has become as much the middle-class party as the Liberal used to be, as much and more.

The sleek citizens, who pour forth daily from thousands and thousands of smug villas round London, Manchester and Liverpool, read their Standard and believe that the country will do very well as it is.... Conservatism has opened its arms to the middle-classes, and has reaped its just reward....

This, then, appears to us the great lesson of the elections of 1874, that the middle-classes have gone over to the enemy bag and baggage.

From Frederic Harrison, 'The Conservative Reaction', *The Fortnightly Review*, vol. 15, 1874.

document 7

Engels on the General Election of 1868

Engels had a considerable knowledge of English economic and political conditions. Like Marx, however, he was continually disillusioned by the unrevolutionary behaviour of English working-men.

What do you say to the elections in the factory districts? Once again the proletariat has discredited itself terribly. Everywhere the proletariat is the tag, rag and bobtail of the official parties, and if any party has gained strength from the new votes it is the Tories... it remains a disastrous certificate of poverty for the English proletariat all the same. The parson has shown unexpected power and so has the cringing to respectability. Not a single working-class candidate had a ghost of a chance, but my Lord Tumnoddy or any parvenu snob c'd have the workers' votes with pleasure.

Engels to Marx, 18 November 1868.
From *Marx and Engels on Britain*, Moscow 1953.

document 8

Sir John Skelton on Disraeli, 1867

And the potent wizard himself, with his olive complexion and coal-black eyes, and the mighty dome of his forehead (no Christian temple, be sure), is unlike any living creature one has met. I had never seen him in the daylight before, and the daylight accentuates his strangeness. The face is more like a mask than ever, and the division between him and mere mortals more marked. They say, and say truly enough, What an actor the man is! and yet the ultimate impression is of absolute sincerity and unreserve. Grant Duff will have it that he is an alien. What's England to him, or he to England? There is just where they are wrong. Whig or Radical or Tory don't matter much, perhaps; but this mightier Venice – this Imperial Republic on which the sun never sets – that vision fascinates him, or I am much mistaken. England is the Israel of his imagination, and he will be the Imperial Minister before he dies – if he gets the chance.

From G. E. Buckle and W. M. Monypenny, *Life of Benjamin Disraeli, Earl of Beaconsfield*, Murray (2 vols, rev. edn 1929), ii, 292–3.

document 9
Disraeli on Conservative aims

The following is the classical statement of the aims of the Conservative Party under Disraeli, and particularly of his support for social reform. It is worth comparing, however, with **doc. 10**

Gentlemen, I have referred to what I look upon as the first object of the Tory party – namely, to maintain the institutions of the country, and reviewing what has occurred, and referring to the present temper of the times upon these subjects, I think that the Tory party, or, as I will venture to call it, the National party, has everything to encourage it. I think that the nation, tested by many and severe trials, has arrived at the conclusion which we have always maintained, that it is the first duty of England to maintain its institutions, because to them we principally ascribe the power and prosperity of the country. Gentlemen, there is another and second great object of the Tory party. If the first is to maintain the institutions of the country, the second is, in my opinion, to uphold the Empire of England. If you look to the history of this country since the advent of Liberalism – forty years ago – you will find that there has been no effort so continuous, so subtle, supported by so much energy, and carried on with so much ability and acumen, as the attempts of Liberalism to effect the disintegration of the Empire of England. Gentlemen, another great object of the Tory party, and one not inferior to the maintenance of the Empire, or the upholding of our institutions, is the elevation of the condition of the people.

Speech at the Crystal Palace, 24 June 1872.

From *Selected Speeches of the Earl of Beaconsfield*, ed. T. E. Kebbel, vol. ii, 1882.

document 10

Disraeli and social reform

R. A. Cross was Disraeli's Home Secretary 1874–80, and responsible for important social reforms.

When the Cabinet came to discuss the Queen's Speech, I was, I confess, disappointed at the want of originality shown by the Prime Minister. From all his speeches, I had quite expected that his mind was full of legislative schemes, but such did not prove to be the case; on the contrary, he had to rely on the various suggestions of his colleagues, and as they themselves had only just come into office, and that suddenly, there was some difficulty in framing the Queen's Speech.

From Viscount Cross, *A Political History* (quoted **56**, p. 199).

document 11

Gladstone on the evils of 'Beaconsfieldism'

The following is typical of much of Gladstone's oratory during the Mid-lothian Campaign 1879–80. Disraeli's Government had engaged in wars against the Zulus in South Africa, and the Afghans, in 1879.

Go from South Africa to the mountains of Central Asia. Go into the lofty hills of Afghanistan, as they were last winter, and what do we there see? I fear a yet sadder sight than was to be seen in the land of the Zulus.... You have seen during last winter from time to time that from such and such a village attacks had been made upon the British forces, and that in consequence the village had been burned. Have you ever reflected on the meaning of those words?... Those hill tribes had committed no real offence against us. We, in the pursuit of our political objects, chose to establish military positions in their country. If they resisted, would not you have done the same? And when, going forth from their villages they had resisted, what you find is this, that those who went forth were slain, and that the village is burned. Again, I say, have you considered the meaning of these words? The meaning of the burning of the village is, that the women and the children were driven forth to perish in the snows of winter. Is not that a terrible supposition? Is not that a fact which ... rouses in you a sentiment of horror and grief, to think that the name of England, under no political necessity, but for a war as frivolous as ever was waged in the history of man, should be associated with consequences such as these? ...

Remember the rights of the savage, as we call him. Remember that the happiness of his humble home, remember that the sanctity of life in the hill villages of Afghanistan among the winter snows, is as inviolable in the eye of Almighty God as can be your own.

Speech at the Forsters Hall, Dalkeith, 26 November 1879. From W. E. Gladstone, *Political Speeches in Scotland, November and December, 1879*, Edinburgh 1880.

document 12

An old-time election agent

Mr Acland dabbled in all sorts of election work. He was an adept at Election addresses. He knew how to say nothing and to say it well. None of his candidates could be convicted of breaking election pledges after their election. In the pursuit of his profession he was not always on one side; I found him out on one occasion nicely. He was Tory agent for Worcester: one of his lieutenants was agent for Droitwich, but Acland pulled the strings. I made speeches against him in both constituencies, but Acland's men won ... He was free and generous to a fault. He could never save money, however much he earned. ... He was a willing helper without fee or reward when the person wanting help was too poor to pay. But as regards the rich candidate, who had his own game to play, he felt justified in spoiling the Egyptians. But he never sold his Candidate; never relaxed his efforts to get him returned. The system was corrupt; that was not his fault. He advocated a better system. Parliament refused it. The candidates liked the system; why should he complain. He lived to see the change: hustings abolished, open voting driven away with the ballot carried and the Corrupt Practices Acts amended and strengthened.

(Quoted **85**, p. 238.)

document 13

The work of a chief whip, 1867

Glyn was Liberal Chief Whip between 1867 and 1873, following the passing of the Second Reform Act. His letter illustrates difficulties, especially financial, that faced party officials under the new electoral conditions.

'The claims upon a Fund' are as follows.

1st Registration. We have an office in London with a Secretary etc. in communication with all the local agents, giving them advice, supplying them with all forms of claims etc. etc., also doing most important work at an election in looking up the outvoters. This is supposed to be kept alive by annual subscriptions but I find £300 a year is all I get towards an expense of near £1500. I have kept this up this year as it would have been most foolish to lose all this perfect machinery (the only basis of organization which we have) upon the eve of a General election. Hayter says it costs more than it is worth but Brand has been a strong advocate for it, & I certainly now find it most necessary. I am sure we have saved thousands of votes by the information & instructions sent to local agents from our headquarters.

The 2nd expense is The Office here which it is needful to have for some months before an election, & if any one sees [? how] the daily work here runs, the visits of candidates & agents & the correspondence & telegraphs upon matters of candidates the necessity for such a 'house of call' cd. not be doubted.

The fund is wanted 3rdly for aid in some cases towards local registration & in some degree for expenses of meetings etc. to rouse popular feeling which can only be done by sending men down to aid candidates etc. etc.

4thly for direct assistance to candidates & of course here, when the money is gone, I cannot tell exactly how it goes but it is given to the candidate & upon the understanding that it is in aid of legitimate expenditure. There are many places where special men are necessary & sometimes such men may have a little less money to spend than the place will fairly cost.... I don't think it possible to manage properly without say £10000 to £15000.

Glyn to Gladstone, 12 September 1867 (quoted **92**).

document 14
The Conservative Central Office, 1880

Compared with **doc. 13** *this shows clearly the enormous advance made in central party organisation since 1867.*

ORDINARY WORK OF CONSERVATIVE CENTRAL OFFICE
Registration. Enquiries are made as to the residence and qualifications of the outvoters of all counties in England & Wales. Forms, instructions & advice are furnished to both Counties and Boroughs.
Elections. Local leaders are assisted in finding suitable candidates. Forms, instructions, and election literature is supplied.
County outvoters are canvassed.
Organization. Formation of new Associations is promoted and assisted. Model rules &c. are supplied. An annual list of clubs & associations is compiled.
Meetings. The continual holding of small local meetings is advised and encouraged. Speakers and hints for speeches are provided. Special meetings (as for example on the Irish question) are from time to time recommended and promoted.
Publications. Pamphlets & Leaflets on current political topics are issued: important speeches are reprinted and circulated.
Press. A weekly publication, called the 'Editors' Handysheet', is issued to provide materials for political articles to the Conservative Provincial Press. Political telegrams are sent from the Lobby to several provincial papers.
Parliamentary. All Bills affecting the interests of the party are circulated amongst the local leaders. Petitions are from time to time promoted.
Statistics. Facts respecting elections, Parliamentary & municipal, are collected and tabulated. An index of political events during the past 10 years is in course of formation.
Correspondence. Enquiries are answered upon such subjects as Finance, Foreign Affairs, Army & Navy administration, Election statistics & procedure, India, Irish affairs, Licensing, Education, Friendly Societies, &c. &c.
Interviews. People of every class call at the office on political business, and every endeavour is made to treat them with courtesy & consideration.

Visits. Constituencies are visited by emissaries from the Central Office of two sorts:

(a) Experienced agents to advise on the registration & electoral machinery.

(b) Gentlemen to stir up dormant constituencies, & recommend local organisation & effort.

J. A. Gorst to Disraeli, 24 February 1881 (quoted **99**, p. 151).

document 15

J. A. Gorst on the Conservative Party

J. A. Gorst brilliantly reorganised the Conservative Party machine in the 1870s; but he felt that his efforts were insufficiently rewarded by the party leaders. The following extract illustrates not only his 'Tory Democracy', but personal pique.

If the Tory party is to continue to exist as a power in the State, it must become a popular party. A mere coalition with the Whig aristocracy might delay, but could not avert its downfall. The days are past when an exclusive class, however great its ability, wealth, and energy, can command a majority in the electorate. The liberties and interests of the people at large are the only things which it is now possible to conserve: the rights of property, the Established Church, the House of Lords, and the Crown itself must be defended on the ground that they are institutions necessary or useful to the preservation of civil and religious liberty and securities for personal freedom, and can be maintained only so far as the people take this view of their subsistence. Unfortunately for Conservatism, its leaders belong solely to one class; they are a clique composed of members of the aristocracy, land-owners, and adherents whose chief merit is subserviency. The party chiefs live in an atmosphere in which a sense of their own importance and of the importance of their class interests and privileges is exaggerated, and to which the opinions of the common people can scarcely penetrate. They are surrounded by sycophants who continually offer up the incense of personal flattery under the pretext of conveying political information. They half fear and half despise the common people, whom they see only through this deceptive medium; they regard them more as dangerous allies to be coaxed and cajoled than as comrades fighting for a common cause.

From 'Conservative disorganisation', *The Fortnightly Review*, vol. 32, 1882.

document 16

Lord Randolph Churchill on Mr Gladstone

This, and the following extract [**doc. 17**], *illustrate Lord Randolph's wit and eloquence as an orator. Clearly, he was better at destruction (and Gladstone was the perfect foil) than construction.*

'Vanity of vanities,' says the preacher, 'all is vanity!' 'Humbug of humbugs,' says the Radical, 'all is humbug.' Gentlemen, we live in an age of advertisement, the age of Holloway's pills, of Colman's mustard, and of Horniman's pure tea; and the policy of lavish advertisement has been so successful in commerce that the Liberal party, with its usual enterprise, had adapted it to politics. The Prime Minister is the greatest living master of the art of personal political advertisement. Holloway, Colman, and Horniman are nothing compared with him. Every act of his, whether it be for the purposes of health, or of recreation, or of religious devotion, is spread before the eyes of every man, woman and child in the United Kingdom on large and glaring placards. For the purposes of an autumn holiday a large transatlantic steamer is specially engaged, the Poet Laureate adorns the suite and receives a peerage as his reward, and the incidents of the voyage are luncheon with the Emperor of Russia and tea with the Queen of Denmark. For the purposes of recreation he has selected the felling of trees; and we may usefully remark that his amusements, like his politics, are essentially destructive. Every afternoon the whole world is invited to assist at the crashing fall of some beech or elm or oak. The forest laments, in order that Mr Gladstone may perspire...

From Speech at Blackpool, 24 January 1884 (quoted in *Speeches of Lord Randolph Churchill*, ed. L. J. Jennings, Longmans 1889 i, 111–12).

Tory Democracy

The Whigs are a class with the prejudices and the vices of a class; the Radicals are a sect with the tyranny and the fanaticism of a sect. . . . The Whigs tell you that the institutions of this kingdom, as illustrated by the balance of Queen, Lords, and Commons, and the Established Church, are but conveniences and useful commodities, which may be safely altered, modified, or even abolished, so long as the alteration, modification or abolition is left to the Whigs to carry out. The Radicals tell you that these institutions are hideous, poisonous and degrading, and that the divine Caucus is the only machine which can turn out, as if it was a patent medicine, the happiness of humanity. But the Tories, who are of the people, know and exclaim that these institutions, which are not so much the work of the genius of man, but rather the inspired offspring of Time, are the tried guarantees of individual liberty, popular government, and Christian morality; that they are the only institutions which possess the virtue of stability, of stability even through all ages; that the harmonious fusion of classes and interests which they represent corresponds with and satisfies the highest aspirations either of peoples or of men; that by them has our Empire been founded and extended in the past; and that by them alone can it prosper or be maintained in the future. Such is the Tory party and such are its principles, by which it can give to England the government she requires – democratic, aristocratic, Parliamentary, monarchical, uniting in an indissoluble embrace religious liberty and social order.

Speech at Blackpool, 24 January 1884 (quoted **60**, p. 230).

The National Liberal Federation

*This, and the following two documents [**19, 20**], illustrate views within the Liberal Party of the 'caucus system', which may be said to date from the formation of the National Liberal Federation in 1877. Lord Hartington, the leading Whig, was at this time leader of the party.*

The Federation is designed to assist the formation of Liberal Associations, on a popular representative basis, throughout the country; to bring such organisations into union, so that by this means the opinions of Liberals, on measures to be supported or resisted, may be readily and authoritatively ascertained; and to aid in concentrating upon the promotion of reforms found to be generally desired the whole force, strength, and resources of the Liberal Party.

The essential feature of the proposed Federation is the principle which must henceforth govern the action of Liberals as a political party – namely, the direct participation of all members of the party in the direction of its policy, and in the selection of those particular measures of reform and of progress to which priority shall be given. This object can be secured only by the organisation of the party upon a representative basis; that is, by popularly elected committees of local associations, and by the union of such local associations, by means of their freely chosen representatives, in a general federation.

From *Proceedings Attending the Formation of the National Federation of Liberal Associations*, Birmingham 1877.

document 19

Chamberlain on the Caucus

The opponents of the Caucus are not to be convinced – they hate it for its virtues – because it puts aside and utterly confounds all that club management and Pall Mall selection which has been going on for so long and which has made of the Lib Party the molluscous, boneless, nerveless thing it is. The Caucus is force, enthusiasm, zeal, activity, movement, popular will and the rule of the majority – the Seven Deadly Sins in fact.

Chamberlain to John Morley, 29 September 1878 (quoted **26**, i, 262).

document 20

Lord Hartington on the National Liberal Federation

I do not feel at all certain that we ought to give in our adhesion to this federation scheme. The Birmingham plan is perhaps the only one on which the Liberal party can be sufficiently organised in a great constituency; and I do not know whether there is much or any objection to its being extended to others. But it is almost certain to put the management into the hands of the most advanced men, because they are the most active. And when we come to a federation of these associations, it seems to me that it will come before long to placing the chief control and direction of the party in the hands of these men, to the exclusion of the more moderate and easy-going Liberals. There is a good deal of the American caucus system about it, which I think is not much liked here; and though we have all been preaching organisation, I think we may sacrifice too much to it.

Lord Hartington to Lord Granville, 23 November 1877 (quoted **22**, i, 245).

document 21

The 'Unauthorised Programme'

This extract is typical of Joseph Chamberlain's early speeches during his campaign for the 'Unauthorised Programme' (so called because it did not have the backing of Gladstone and the party leadership) in 1885. Its attack on property rights shows why Lord Salisbury denounced him as 'Jack Cade'. But in fact Chamberlain modified his ideas in the course of the campaign.

We have to account for and to grapple with the mass of misery and destitution in our midst, coexistent as it is with the evidence of abundant wealth and teeming prosperity. It is a problem which some men would put aside by references to the eternal laws of supply and demand, to the necessity of freedom of contract, and to the sanctity of every private right of property. But, gentlemen, these phrases are the convenient cant of selfish wealth. They are no answers to our question. I quite understand the reason for timidity in dealing with this matter so long as Government was merely the expression of the will and prejudice of a limited few. Under such circumstances there might be good reason for not intrusting it with larger powers, even for the relief of this misery and destitution. But now that we have a Government of the people by the people, we will go on and make it the Government for the people, in which all shall cooperate in order to secure to every man his natural rights, his right to existence, and to a fair enjoyment of it. I shall be told tomorrow that this is Socialism. I have learnt not to be afraid of words that are flung in my face instead of argument. Of course it is Socialism. The Poor Law is Socialism; the Education Act is Socialism; the greater part of municipal work is Socialism; and every kindly act of legislation, by which the community has sought to discharge its responsibilities and its obligations to the poor is Socialism; but it is none the worse for that. Our object is the elevation of the poor, of the masses of the people – a levelling up of them by which we shall do something to remove the excessive inequality in social life which is now one of the greatest dangers as well as a great injury to the State.

Speech at Warrington, 8 September 1885.
From *Speeches of Right Hon. Joseph Chamberlain, M.P.* ed. H. W. Lucy, 1885.

document 22
Gladstone and Irish nationality

It was during the summer months of 1885 that Gladstone, privately, became converted to the necessity for Home Rule for Ireland. A major reason for this was his growing conviction of the reality of Irish nationalism, and his belief that his previous policies of reform and coercion had failed. This may be compared with Chamberlain's views [doc. 23]; *and the light thrown on his attitude towards the Home Rule Bill of 1886 by* doc. 24.

He (Gladstone) said he had been studying the subject a good deal; that he had come to the conclusion that the Union was a mistake; that Pitt had assigned no sufficient justification for destroying the national life of Ireland; that he did not hold the popular theory that a single executive could not co-exist with two independent legislatures (witness Norway and Sweden, Austria and Hungary); he did not believe the Irish irreconcilable; thought they would have accepted moderate terms till R. Churchill came into power; now nothing less than a Parliament of their own would satisfy them; the question was becoming urgent; the Irish were better organised than ever; we could not go on with eighty or ninety of them in the House of Commons – the state of that body now was a disgrace, and it would be worse in the new Parliament.

Lord Derby to Earl Granville, 2 October 1885 (quoted 26, vol. ii, p. iii).

document 23
Chamberlain on Ireland

I hate coercion; but I loathe violence and disorder more. I do not judge the morality of Irish proceedings but I recognise facts. We are in a state of war, and I will use every conceivable means to come out victorious. They mean to destroy the Government, and perhaps in this they may be successful. They want also to make all government of Ireland by England impossible, and in this they will assuredly fail, as all our people, Radicals included, will resist them to the death.

Chamberlain to John Morley, 18 December 1881 (quoted **26**, ii, 345).

document 24

Chamberlain and Home Rule

The immediate result will be considerable unpopularity and temporary estrangement from the Radical Party. There is little backbone in politics and the great majority are prepared to swallow anything and to stick to the machine. In the Cabinet I have no support worth mentioning. . . . I shall be left almost alone for a time. I cannot, of course, work with the Tories, and Hartington is quite as much hostile to my radical views as to W.G.'s Irish plans. But in time the situation will clear. Either Mr. Gladstone will succeed and get the Irish question out of the way, or he will fail. In either case he will retire from politics and I do not suppose the Liberal Party will accept Childers or even John Morley as its permanent leader.

Joseph Chamberlain to Arthur Chamberlain, 8 March 1886 (quoted **82**).

document 25

The working class and Liberalism

Sidney Webb was at this time a young civil servant, active in London politics. The view expressed is probably true of the whole period 1886 to 1900.

The general tone of mind and bias of character of the London wage-earner is emphatically Radical. Nevertheless it is by no means uncommon for them to vote by hundreds for the Conservative candidate, partly from sheer disgust at the weakness of Liberalism, partly no doubt because of specious 'Tory Democratic' promises, but mainly for personal or accidental reasons. . . . Their usual attitude, however, is abstention; first from registration; then, if registered, perforce, from the polling-booth. Practically none of them give any assistance in ordinary times to the necessary work of a

Liberal Association. Even such of them as can be induced at the election to vote for the Liberal candidate, are in the party but not of it. There is an almost universal conviction among them that its aims are not theirs, and that its representatives are not those whom they would have chosen.

From Sidney Webb, *Wanted a Programme: An Appeal to the Liberal Party, 1888* (quoted from Simon Maccoby, *English Radicalism 1886–1914*, Allen & Unwin 1953, pp. 58–9).

document 26

Gladstone's last Cabinet

The Earl of Kimberley was, in 1895, Foreign Secretary, and had served in Liberal governments continuously since 1868. The Chancellor of the Exchequer was Sir William Harcourt.

On March 1 Mr Gladstone held his last Cabinet. After the business was concluded Kimberley said that he could not allow our meeting to terminate without saying in a word how painful it was for us to part with our chief, and in a moment the honest old fellow was sobbing, unable to proceed. Mr G. was about to reply when a cry of 'Stop!' was heard. It was the Chancellor of the Exchequer. As soon as he had arrested Mr G's attention he pulled from his pocket a handkerchief and a manuscript and at once commenced weeping loudly. Then he said, 'I think I can best express my feelings by reading the letter I have addressed to you, Sir, on this occasion' – on which he declaimed to us a somewhat pompous valedictory address of which I only remember vaguely a long-drawn metaphor taken from the solar system. Mr Gladstone was obviously disgusted. He said a few cold words, and always referred to this Cabinet as 'the blubbering Cabinet'.

From the Earl of Rosebery, *Mr Gladstone's Last Cabinet* (**36**).

document 27

Rosebery's position as Prime Minister

The Liberal Government of 1892–95 was dependent for its parliamentary majority on the Irish Party. The leader of the Liberal Party in the House of Commons was Sir William Harcourt, previously Rosebery's rival for the succession to Gladstone, and his personal enemy.

He is as Prime Minister more unfortunately situated than any man who ever held that high office. He has inherited from his predecessor a policy, a Cabinet, and a Parliament; besides a party of groups, one of which is aimed against himself. All this is kept in existence by a narrow majority which may at any moment break away. He himself is only able to guide this tumultuous party through a leader, bitterly hostile to himself, and ostentatiously indifferent to the fate of the Government.

Lord Rosebery in the meantime is shut up in a House almost unanimously opposed to his ministry, and, for all political purposes, might as well be in the Tower of London.

Earl of Rosebery to Queen Victoria, 14 May 1894 (quoted **4**, pp. 71–2).

document 28

Asquith on the Liberal Party, 1898

Asquith was Home Secretary 1892–95; and though his political sympathies lay more with Rosebery than Harcourt, his view of the Liberal Party is reasonably objective. He was himself a possible candidate for the party leadership in 1898 after the retirement of Harcourt.

The new birth has not yet come, nor is there anything in the heavens above or in the earth beneath to portend the event. Harcourt's leadership excites no enthusiasm, and, in view of his age & of the other conditions, is probably regarded by the bulk of the people as a merely provisional arrangement. There is a disposition – I think a growing one – to turn to Rosebery, but there are many who cannot forget or forgive his timely escape, in a life-boat constructed to hold one person, from the water-logged ship. And for the moment there is no one else whose name is even generally acceptable, let alone a rallying cry for a broken army. The fact is that people have been so accustomed for more than a generation upon both sides to leaders who are obviously marked out for the post (Palmerston, Gladstone, Disraeli, Salisbury) that they are bewildered by the problem of choice. In the end it will no doubt solve itself by the action of natural forces, but in the meantime the effectiveness of the party as a political instrument is crippled.

H. H. Asquith to Alfred Milner, January 1898 (quoted **37**, p. 234).

Labour and the Caucus

Threlfall was a trade union leader and active worker for greater labour representation in Parliament. His views are typical of those of many labour leaders in the later nineteenth century.

Theoretically the caucus is a perfect machine, but in practice it is one-sided... It is only a waste of time to advise the working classes to attend and make the caucus what they want it to be. The fact is they distrust it – they regard it as a middle-class machine; they have neither the time nor the inclination to compete with the wire-pullers who work it, and they have a decided objection to being made the puppets of anyone. It has served its purpose, and it has carried the people through one state of their development: but as it exists today it is too narrow and too much hampered with class prejudice to be a reflex of the expanding democratic and labour sentiment.

T. R. Threlfall in *The Nineteenth Century*, February 1894 (quoted **127**, pp. 222–3).

Salisbury on Lord Randolph Churchill, 1886

Lord Cranbrook, Lord President of the Council, complained to Salisbury about his undue regard for Churchill's opinions. The Prime Minister's reply reveals his true feelings.

What you call my self-renunciation is merely an effort to deal with an abnormal and very difficult state of things. It arises from the peculiarities of Churchill. Beach having absolutely refused to lead, Churchill is the only possible leader in the House of Commons – and his ability is unquestionable. But he is wholly out of sympathy with the rest of the Cabinet, and, being besides of a wayward and headstrong disposition, he is far from mitigating his resistance by the method of it. As his office of Leader of the House gives him a claim to be heard on every question, the machine is moving along with the utmost friction both in home and foreign affairs. My self-renunciation is only an attempt – a vain attempt – to pour oil upon the creaking and groaning machinery. Like you, I am penetrated with a sense of the danger which the collapse of the Government would bring about: otherwise I should not have undertaken – or should have quickly abandoned – the task of leading an orchestra in which the first fiddle plays one tune and everybody else, including myself, wishes to play another.

Lord Salisbury to Lord Cranbrook, November 1886 (quoted **61**, p. 277).

document 31
The Liberal Unionist Party

This extract from Joseph Chamberlain's Political Memoir, *(written mainly in 1892 in defence of his policies over the previous ten years) well illustrates his difficulties as a Liberal Unionist after 1887.*

All attempts at reconciliation and the reunion of the Liberal Party having now failed, the next few years, from 1888 till the General Election of 1892, were occupied in maintaining and strengthening the Unionist alliance. The situation was extremely difficult – especially at first. The Conservative Party had their old traditions and methods and were inclined to move slowly or not at all. Lord Hartington, who in 1885 had been the most moderate of Whigs, found little difficulty in accepting a negative policy. He showed no initiative and was inclined on all occasions to wait for the Tory lead and at the same time was most destructive in his criticisms of all new proposals and policies. On the other hand the Liberal Unionists in the country were restive at the idea of working with, and especially under, new allies. They had been accustomed to look on all that bore the name, or was connected with the idea, of Toryism as altogether unacceptable and detestable. They were determined not to sacrifice their Liberalism, and were pledged to reforms which they had hitherto been accustomed to identify with the Liberal Party. Unless this important section of Liberals, whose sole difference with Mr Gladstone was the Home Rule question, and who were eager to find a compromise on this, could be kept true, the Gladstonians would speedily outnumber the Conservatives in the country, and would return to power with a majority sufficient to carry their policy. The position of Liberal Unionists in the constituencies was not a pleasant one. They were reviled by their former friends, and did not thoroughly trust, nor were they trusted by, their new allies. They were without efficient organisation, isolated and uneasy; and accordingly many did go back to their old party as the by-elections showed; while others, less strongly Liberal in their convictions, frankly joined the Tories, ceasing to call themselvevs Liberals at all.

(Quoted **29**, pp. 276–7.)

document **32**
Chamberlain on the socialist menace

This extract shows how far Chamberlain had travelled in his social and political views since 1885. It may be compared with **doc. 21**.

Information obtained from a great number of constituencies ... and confirmed by other correspondence, shows that the electors are much more interested at the present time in social questions and the problems connected with the agitations of the Labour Party than they are in either the House of Lords or any other constitutional subject. There is much more searching of heart among the most moderate, and above all the wealthier Gladstonians. The men who have anything to lose are getting uneasy now that they see that Gladstonianism is not likely to be confined to an attack upon Irish landlords or British millionaires, but will probably result in an onslaught on capital generally.

The resolutions of the TUC ... amount to universal confiscation in order to create a Collectivist State. It is true that this is at present an unauthorised programme, but the policy of the Gladstonian leaders has been, and still is, to invite popular pressure in order that they may yield to it ... in doing so, they will risk a further secession of all that remains to them of wealth, intelligence, and moderation.

From Joseph Chamberlain, *Memorandum*, November 1894 (quoted **80**, pp. 64–5).

document **33**
The 'Hotel Cecil'

Salisbury's last ministry contained two of his nephews – Gerald and Arthur Balfour – hence the nickname of the 'Hotel Cecil'. Bartley had been Conservative Party Agent 1882–85.

It becomes clearer after every appointment that though men may work their hearts out and make every sacrifice financial and otherwise when the Conservative party is in opposition and in difficulties, yet in prosperous times all is forgotten and all honours, emoluments and places are reserved for the friends and relations of the favoured few, many of whom were in the nursery while some of us were fighting uphill battles for the party.

G. C. T. Bartley to Lord Salisbury, 22 October 1898 (quoted **64**).

document 34

Lord Salisbury on the Conservative Party

Salisbury's reply to Lord Randolph Churchill's demand for a more vigorous reform policy illustrates perfectly his slow, cautious, sceptical view of political change.

For the rest, I fully see all the difficulties of our position. The Tory party is composed of very varying elements, and there is merely trouble and vexation of spirit in trying to make them work together. I think the 'classes and the dependants of class' are the strongest ingredients in our composition, but we have so to conduct our legislation that we shall give some satisfaction to both classes and masses. This is specially difficult with the classes – because all legislation is rather unwelcome to them, as tending to disturb a state of things with which they are satisfied. It is evident, therefore, that we must work at less speed and at a lower temperature than our opponents. Our Bills must be tentative and cautious, not sweeping and dramatic. But I believe that with patience, feeling our way as we go, we may yet get the one element to concede and the other to forbear. The opposite course is to produce drastic, symmetrical measures, hitting the 'classes' hard, and consequently dispensing with their support, but trusting to public meetings and the democratic forces generally to carry you through. I think such a policy will fail. I do not mean that the 'classes' will join issue with you on one of the measures which hits them hard, and beat you on that. That is not the way they fight. They will select some other matter on which they can appeal to prejudice, and on which they think the masses will be indifferent; and on that they will upset you.

Lord Salisbury to Lord Randolph Churchill, 7 November 1886 (quoted **60**, p. 565).

Bibliography

GENERAL

1 Kitson Clark, G. *An Expanding Society. Britain 1830–1900*, Cambridge University Press, 1967.

2 Ensor, R. C. K. *England 1870–1914*, Oxford University Press, 1936: the standard textbook – and a very good one – now somewhat out of date.

3 Halévy, Elie. *Imperialism and the Rise of Labour 1895–1905: A history of the English people in the nineteenth century*, vol. v, Benn, 1926: an illuminating detailed study by a great historian.

4 Hanham, H. J. *The Nineteenth Century Constitution. Documents and Commentary*, Cambridge University Press, 1969: almost the only documentary collection that covers this period.

5 Beales, Derek. *From Castlereagh to Gladstone 1815–1885*, Nelson, 1969.

6 Read, Donald. *England 1868–1914: The Age of Urban Democracy*, Longman, 1979.

7 Shannon, Richard. *The Crisis of Imperialism 1865–1915*, Hart-Davis, McGibbon, 1974; Paladin edn, 1976: strong on ideas.

For the earlier Victorian period:

8 Kitson Clark, G. *The Making of Victorian England*, Methuen, 1962.

9 Burn, W. L. *The Age of Equipoise*, Allen & Unwin, 1964.

10 Bagehot, Walter. *The English Constitution*, 2nd edn, 1872; Oxford University Press, 1928: a classic study of the mid-Victorian constitution.

11 Smith, F. B. *The Making of the Second Reform Bill*, Cambridge University Press, 1966.

12 Cowling, Maurice, *1867: Disraeli, Gladstone and Revolution*, Cambridge University Press, 1967.

THE LIBERAL PARTY

13 Vincent, John. *The Formation of the Liberal Party 1857–1868*, Constable 1965: a brilliant, stimulating and exasperating book.

14 Williams, W. E. *The Rise of Gladstone to the Leadership of The Liberal Party 1859–1868*, Cambridge University Press, 1934.

15 Morley, John. *Life of Gladstone*, 2 vols, Macmillan, 1905 edn.

16 Magnus, Philip. *Gladstone*, Murray, 1954: the best modern life.

17 Thompson, A. F. 'Gladstone', *History Today*, November 1952: a hostile view.

18 Ramm, Agatha, ed. *The Political Correspondence of Mr Gladstone and Lord Granville 1876–1886*, 2 vols, Oxford University Press, 1962: contains a valuable introduction.

19 Adams, Francis. *History of the Elementary School Contest in England*, Chapman & Hall, 1882: important for the 'Nonconformist Revolt'.

20 Glaser, John F. 'English nonconformists and the decline of Liberalism', *American Historical Review*, vol. 63, 1957–58.

21 Southgate, Donald. *The Passing of the Whigs 1832–1886*, Macmillan, 1962: together with **22** it provides a full-dress portrait of the Whig Section of the Liberal Party.

22 Holland, Bernard. *The Life of Spencer Compton, 8th Duke of Devonshire*, 2 vols, Longmans, 1911.

23 Shannon, R. T. *Gladstone and the Bulgarian Agitation 1876*, Nelson, 1963: an outstanding book, with wider implications than its title suggests.

24 Beckett, J. C. *The Making of Modern Ireland 1603–1923*, Faber, 1966.

25 Hammond, J. L. *Gladstone and the Irish Nation* (1st edn, 1938), Cass, 1964: the standard work – very pro-Gladstone.

26 Garvin, J. L. and Amery, Julian. *Life of Joseph Chamberlain*, 6 vols, Macmillan, 1932–69: the standard life.

27 Fraser, Peter. *Joseph Chamberlain*, Cassell, 1966: interesting on some aspects of Chamberlain, but on the whole an unsuccessful attempt to provide a modern one-volume life.

28 Howard, C. H. D. 'Joseph Chamberlain and the "Unauthorised Programme" ', *English Historical Review*, vol. 65, 1950.

29 Chamberlain, Joseph. *A Political Memoir 1880–92*, ed. C. H. D. Howard, Batchworth Press, 1953: an apologia.

30 Chamberlain, Joseph. Preface to *The Radical Programme*, 1885.

31 Chamberlain, Joseph. 'The Liberal Party and its leaders', *Fortnightly Review*, vol. 14, 1873.

32 Escott, T. H. S. 'The revolution of 1884', *Fortnightly Review*, vol. 37, 1885.

33 Hamer, D. A. *John Morley. Liberal Intellectual in Politics*, Oxford

University Press, 1968.

34 Butler, Jeffrey. *The Liberal Party and the Jameson Raid*, Oxford University Press, 1968.

35 James, R. R. *Rosebery*, Weidenfeld & Nicolson, 1963.

36 Rosebery, Earl of. 'Mr Gladstone's last cabinet', *History Today*, Dec. 1951 and Jan. 1952: an important contemporary document.

37 Stansky, Peter. *Ambitions and Struggles. The Struggle for the leadership of the Liberal Party in the 1890's*, Oxford University Press, 1964: a detailed study of the 'in-fighting' – only for addicts.

38 Wilson, Trevor. *The Downfall of the Liberal Party 1914–1935*, Collins (Fontana Library edn.), 1968; contains an important introduction on the general problem of Liberal decline.

39 Barker, Michael. *Gladstone and Radicalism. The Reconstruction of Liberal Policy in Britain 1885–1894*, The Harvester Press, 1975.

40 Cooke, A. B. and Vincent, John. *The Governing Passion. Cabinet Government and Party Politics in Britain 1885–86*, The Harvester Press, 1974: a study of 'high (often stratospheric) politics.'

41 Cook, Chris. *A Short History of the Liberal Party 1900–1976*, Macmillan, 1976.

42 Clarke, P. F. *Lancashire and the New Liberalism*, Cambridge University Press, 1971.

43 Douglas, Roy. *History of the Liberal Party 1895–1970*, Sidgwick and Jackson, 1971.

44 Emy, H. V. *Liberals, Radicals and Social Politics 1892–1914*, Cambridge University Press, 1973.

45 Feuchtwanger, E. J. *Gladstone*, Allen Lane, 1975.

46 Hamer, D. A. *Liberal Politics in the Age of Gladstone and Rosebery*, Oxford University Press, 1972: the outstanding study of the late Victorian Liberal Party.

47 Judd, Denis. *Radical Joe. A Life of Joseph Chamberlain*, Hamish Hamilton, 1977: now the best short life.

48 Lyons, F. S. L. *Ireland since the Famine*, Weidenfeld and Nicolson, 1971.

49 Morgan, Kenneth O. *The Age of Lloyd George. The Liberal Party and British Politics 1890–1929*, Allen and Unwin, 1971.

50 Matthew, H. C. G., ed. *The Gladstone Diaries*, vol. V, 1855–1860, Oxford University Press, 1978: contains an illuminating introduction.

51 McCready, H. W. 'Home Rule and the Liberal Party 1899–1906', *Irish Historical Studies*, 13, 1962–3.

52 Steele, E. D. 'Gladstone and Ireland', *Irish Historical Studies*, 17, 1970–1.

53 Matthew, H. C. G. The *Liberal Imperialists*, Oxford University Press, 1973.

54 Adelman, Paul. *The Decline of the Liberal Party 1910–1931*, Seminar Studies in History, Longman, 1982.

THE CONSERVATIVE PARTY

55 Blake, Robert. *Disraeli*, Methuen, 1966: one of the outstanding political biographies of our time.

56 Smith, Paul. *Disraelian Conservatism and Social Reform*, Routledge, 1967: a first-class study of a neglected theme.

57 Cecil, Robert, 'The Past and Future of Conservative Policy', *Quarterly Review*, vol. 127, Oct. 1869.

58 Lewis, Clyde J. 'Theory and expediency in the policy of Disraeli', *Victorian Studies*, vol. 4, 1960–61.

59 McDowell, R. B. *British Conservatism 1832–1914*, Faber, 1959: one of the few general studies – good on ideas.

60 Churchill, W. S. *Lord Randolph Churchill* (1st edn, 1906), Odhams Press edn, 1952.

61 James, Robert Rhodes. *Lord Randolph Churchill*, Weidenfeld & Nicolson, 1959: a fine modern biography, admirably complements **60**.

62 Howard, C. H. D. 'Lord Randolph Churchill', *History*, vol. 25, June 1940: hostile.

63 Cornford, J. P. 'The transformation of Conservatism in the late 19th century', *Victorian Studies*, vol. 7, 1963–64: an outstanding article.

64 Cornford, J. P. 'The parliamentary foundations of the Hotel Cecil', in *Ideas and Institutions of Victorian England*, ed. Robert Robson, Bell, 1967.

65 Dunbabin, J. P. D. 'The politics of the establishment of county councils', *The Historical Journal*, vol. 6, 1963.

66 Chilston, Viscount. *Chief Whip. The Political Life and Times of Aretas Akers-Douglas, 1st Viscount Chilston*, Routledge, 1961: this work and **67** give an excellent account of the internal workings of the Conservative Party in the later nineteenth century.

67 Chilston, Viscount. *W. H. Smith*, Routledge, 1965.

68 Cecil, Lady Gwendolen. *Life of Robert, Marquis of Salisbury*, 4 vols, Hodder & Stoughton, 1921–32: the standard biography, but only reaches 1892.

69 Blake, Robert. *The Conservative Party from Peel to Churchill*, Eyre and Spottiswoode, 1970.

70 Curtis, L. P. Jr. *Coercion and Conciliation in Ireland 1880–1892*, Princeton University Press, 1962.

71 Elridge, C. C. *England's Mission: the Imperial Idea in the Age of Gladstone and Disraeli 1868–80*, Hodder and Stoughton, 1973.

72 Harcourt, Freda. 'Disraeli's Imperialism, 1866–1868: A Question of Timing', *The Historical Journal*, vol. 23, 1980.

73 Marsh, Peter. *The Discipline of Popular Government: Lord Salisbury's Domestic Statecraft, 1881–1902*, The Harvester Press, 1978: a large-scale narrative.

74 Quinault, R. E. 'Lord Randolph Churchill and Tory Democracy, 1880–1885' *The Historical Journal*, vol. 22, 1979.

75 Smith, Paul, ed. *Lord Salisbury on Politics*, Cambridge University Press, 1972: contains a brilliant introduction.

76 Southgate, Donald. 'The Salisbury Era 1881–1902', in *The Conservative Leadership*, ed. Donald Southgate, Macmillan, 1974.

77 Stewart, Robert. *The Foundation of the Conservative Party 1830–1867. A History of the Conservative Party, vol. I*, Longman, 1978.

78 Taylor, Robert. *Lord Salisbury*, Allen Lane, 1975.

79 Ward, J. T. 'Derby and Disraeli', in *The Conservative Leadership*, ed. Donald Southgate, Macmillan, 1974.

LIBERAL UNIONISM

80 Fraser, Peter. 'The Liberal Unionist alliance: Chamberlain, Hartington and the Conservatives 1886–1904', *English Historical Review*, vol. 77, 1962.

81 Goodman, Gordon L. 'Liberal Unionism: the revolt of the Whigs', *Victorian Studies*, vol. 3, 1959.

82 Hurst, M. C. *Joseph Chamberlain and West Midland Politics 1886–1895*. Dugdale Society Occasional Papers No. 15, Oxford University Press, 1962.

83 Hurst, M. C. *Joseph Chamberlain and Liberal Reunion*, Routledge, 1967: important, though difficult.

84 Hurst, M. C. 'Joseph Chamberlain, the Conservatives and the succession to John Bright 1886–1889', *The Historical Journal*, vol. 7, 1964.

ELECTIONS AND PARTY ORGANISATION

85 Hanham, H. J. *Elections and Party Management. Politics in the time of Disraeli and Gladstone*, Longmans, 1959: the most important book for the period up to 1885.

86 Hanham, H. J. *The Reformed Electoral System in Great Britain 1832–1914*, The Historical Association 1968: a good brief outline.

87 Lowell, Lawrence A. *The Government of England*, 2 vols, Macmillan, 1912 edn: a near-contemporary view of the later nineteenth-century constitution.

88 Ostrogorski, M. *Democracy and the Organisation of Political Parties*, vol. 1, England, 1st edn, 1902, edited and abridged by Seymour Martin Lipset, Quadrangle Books, Chicago 1964: a classic study of the rise of mass politics.

89 McKenzie, Robert. *British Political Parties*, 2nd edn, Heinemann, 1963: a modern classic, with important historical sections.

90 Beer, Samuel H. *Modern British Politics*, Faber, 1965.

91 Maehl, W. H. 'Gladstone, the Liberals and the election of 1874', *Bulletin of the Institute of Historical Research*, vol. 36, 1963.

92 Thompson, A. F. 'Gladstone's Whips and the general election of 1868', *English Historical Review*, vol. 63, 1948.

93 McGill, Barry. 'Francis Schnadhorst and Liberal Party organisation', *Journal of Modern History*, vol. 35, 1962.

94 Tholfsen, Trygve R. 'The origins of the Birmingham caucus', *The Historical Journal*, vol. 2, 1959.

95 Herrick, Francis H. 'The origins of the National Liberal Federation', *Journal of Modern History*, vol. 17, 1945.

96 Herrick, Francis H. 'Lord Randolph Churchill and the popular organisation of the Conservative Party', *Pacific Historical Review*, vol. 15, 1946.

97 Chamberlain, Joseph. 'A new political organisation', *Fortnightly Review*, vol. 22, 1877.

98 Howarth, Janet. 'The Liberal revival in Northamptonshire 1880–1895: a case study in late 19th century elections', *The Historical Journal*, vol. 12, 1969.

99 Feuchtwanger, E. J. *Disraeli, Democracy and the Tory Party. Conservative Leadership and Organisation after the Second Reform Bill*, Oxford University Press, 1968.

100 Pelling, Henry. *Social Geography of British Elections 1885–1910*,

Macmillan, 1967: a pioneer study, though its methods have been much criticised.

101 O'Leary, Cornelius. *The Elimination of Corrupt Practices in British Elections 1868–1911*, Oxford University Press, 1962.

102 Seymour, Charles. *Electoral Reform in England and Wales*, Yale University Press, 1915: still the standard work for the period up to 1885.

103 Lloyd, Trevor. *The General Election of 1880*, Oxford University Press, 1968.

104 Lloyd, Trevor. 'Uncontested seats in British general elections 1852–1910', *The Historical Journal*, vol. 8, 1965.

105 Dunbabin, J. P. D. 'Expectations of the new county councils, and their realization', *The Historical Journal*, vol. 8, 1965.

106 Dunbabin, J. P. D. 'Parliamentary elections in Great Britain, 1868–1900: a psephological note', *English Historical Review*, vol. 81, 1966.

107 Blewett, Neal. 'The Franchise in the United Kingdom 1885–1918', *Past and Present*, vol. 32, 1965: of major importance for the post-1885 period.

108 Chadwick, Mary, E. J. 'The Role of Redistribution in the Making of the Third Reform Act', *The Historical Journal*, vol. 19, 1976.

109 Clarke, P. F. 'The Electoral Sociology of Modern Britain', *History*, vol. 57, 1972.

110 Fraser, Derek. *Urban Politics in Victorian England*, Leicester University Press, 1976.

111 Jones, Andrew. *The Politics of Reform 1884*, Cambridge University Press, 1972.

112 Simon, Alan. 'Church Disestablishment as a Factor in the General Election of 1885', *The Historical Journal*, vol. 18, 1975.

113 Vincent, J. R. *Pollbooks: How Victorians Voted*, Cambridge University Press, 1967.

114 Wright, D. G. *Democracy and Reform 1815–1885*, Seminar Studies in History, Longman, 1970.

ECONOMIC AND SOCIAL DEVELOPMENTS

115 Hobsbawm, E. J. *Industry and Empire. An Economic History of Britain since 1750*, Weidenfeld & Nicolson, 1968: a stimulating survey.

116 Thompson, F. M. L. *English Landed Society in the Nineteenth Century*, Routledge, 1963: a major work – indispensable.

Bibliography

117 Thompson, F. M. L. 'Land and Politics in England in the Nineteenth Century', *Transactions of the Royal Historical Society*, vol. 15, 1965.

118 Brown, B. H. *The Tariff Reform Movement in Great Britain 1881–1895*, Columbia University Press, 1943.

119 Ensor, R. C. K. 'Some political and economic interactions in later Victorian England', *Transactions of the Royal Historical Society*, vol. 31, 1949.

120 Pumphrey, Ralph E. 'The introduction of industrialists into the British peerage: a study in adaptation of a social institution', *American Historical Review*, vol. 65, 1959–60.

121 Hanham, H. J. 'The sale of honours in Late Victorian England', *Victorian Studies*, vol. 3, 1959–60.

122 Guttsman, W. L. *The British Political Elite*, MacGibbon & Kee, 1965.

THE LABOUR MOVEMENT

123 Webb, Sidney, and Webb, Beatrice. *The History of Trade Unionism*, 2nd edn, Longmans, 1920.

124 Roberts, B. C. *The Trades Union Congress 1868–1921*, Allen & Unwin, 1958.

125 Clegg, H. A., Fox, Alan, and Thompson, A. F. *A History of British Trade Unionism since 1889*, vol. i: 1889–1910, Oxford University Press, 1964.

126 Harrison, Royden. *Before the Socialists. Studies in Labour and Politics 1861–1881*, Routledge, 1965.

127 Pelling, Henry, *The Origins of the Labour Party 1880–1900*, 2nd edn, Oxford University Press, 1965.

128 Pelling, Henry. *Popular Politics and Society in late Victorian Britain*, Macmillan, 1968: a stimulating series of essays.

129 Bealey, Frank, and Pelling, Henry. *Labour and Politics 1900–1906*, Macmillan, 1958.

130 MacKenzie, Robert, and Silver, Alan. *Angels in Marble: Working class Conservatives in urban England*, Heinemann, 1968.

131 Thompson, Paul. *Socialists, Liberals and Labour. The struggle for London 1885–1914*, Routledge, 1967.

132 McKibbin, Ross. *The Evolution of the Labour Party 1910–24*, Oxford University Press, 1974.

133 Price, Richard. *An Imperial War and the British Working Class*, Routledge, 1972.

Index

Index